Help For Your Visionary Pastor

Jamie Johnson

Help For Your Visionary Pastor
ISBN: Softcover 978-1-960326-01-0
Copyright © 2022 by Jamie Johnson

All rights reserved. No part of this book may be reproduced or transmitted in any form or by any means, electronic or mechanical, including photocopying, recording, or by any information storage and retrieval system, without permission in writing from the publisher.

Parson's Porch Books is an imprint of Parson's Porch *&* Company (PP*&*C) in Cleveland, Tennessee. PP*&*C is a self-funded charity which earns money by publishing books of noted authors, representing all genres. Its face and voice is **David Russell Tullock** (dtullock@parsonsporch.com).

Parson's Porch *&* Company *turns books into bread & milk* by sharing its profits with the poor.

www.parsonsporch.com

Help For Your Visionary Pastor

Contents

Introduction 7
Chapter One 10
   My Personal Journey Leading to Discovery
Chapter Two 17
   More and More; Bigger and Better with Unlimited Resources
Chapter Three 22
   That Sounds Awesome! But Where is the Organization?
Chapter Four 29
   Don't Throw Out the Baby with the Bathwater
Chapter Five 37
   You Keep Popping My Balloon
Chapter Six 42
   Don't Complain; Just Give Me a Solution
Chapter Seven 47
   Feel Free to Criticize, but Please be Constructive
Chapter Eight 57
   Having Prayer Partners I can be Vulnerable Around
Chapter Nine 67
   Becoming More Fond of Delegation
Chapter Ten 72
   Having the Right Team is Essential
Chapter Eleven 79
   Learning to Trust the Process
Chapter Twelve 86
   Learning to Trust in God's Provision
Conclusion 96

Introduction

It was the spring of 2007. My wife, Mindy, was working on her Bachelor's in elementary education, and I worked third shift on an assembly line at a local manufacturing plant. A few evenings every week, after she finished working at the bank, she had to drive to Knoxville (which was about an hour away) to attend class. Our kids were nine and three. Mindy got out of class at 10 pm, and I had to be at work by 10:45. On those days, it was my job to pick the kids up at school and daycare, help my son, Austin, with homework, get them fed, give my daughter, Abby, a bath, and meet Mindy in the town where I worked by 10:40. To say that was challenging for someone like me, would be an understatement.

One of those evenings around 9:45, my phone rang. As soon as I saw that it was my wife, I panicked. She asked me if I was ready to leave, and I told her, "almost." Not exactly correct. The reason for my panic, if I had been completely up front with her, it would have gotten ugly for me. This was my situation at that very moment. Abby was playing in the bathtub, hair full of suds from the shampoo, and there was water heating up on the stove for macaroni and cheese. On the nights Mindy was in class, we always had mac and cheese, and only mac and cheese for dinner. I had picked up my kids around 3:30, yet we were not even ready to leave this late in the evening. What in the world happened?

At this time, I was a youth pastor with a thriving youth group. During my time at this church, we had begun a children's ministry through our students, where we did VBS and Backyard Bible Clubs in underprivileged neighborhoods. We were on the verge of becoming a worldwide ministry, reaching all across the U.S. and other parts of the world.

Around this time, I had been making calls to other states, including California. We had already done some ministry in Montana, but we needed to do more. I was constantly on the phone with someone, talking about the vision I had for this ministry. Time always got away from me. Tonight was one of those nights.

Pretty much, from the time I got home from picking the kids up, until I put Abby in the bath, put on my work clothes, and got the water on the stove to boil, I had been on the telephone talking about this ministry. I was sharing my vision and how we were about to move this ministry from where we were to other states and countries. It was all just wonderful. That is, until the phone rang, and I had to talk to my wife. Those kinds of calls never went well for me.

And, to add insult to injury, the ministry was never ready to go beyond the area we lived in, much less other states and different parts of the world. My problem was I could always see the big picture, but never any of the details. Welcome to my world; that of the visionary pastor.

For 24 years, I have had the opportunity to preach God's Word, and lead people. In all of those years I have led with a strong visionary style. Being a visionary is how God wired me. Leading as an uncontrolled visionary was not really His plan, but that was how I did it for most of my ministry. God has led me to write this book, in order to help those who work under, or beside visionary leaders.

I am taking you on this amazing journey. It began with me not even understanding that there were different leadership styles, to the point that I am learning what I have to do in order to lead effectively. I have had the privilege of serving in several churches. However, for this book, I am only going to share stories from two of those.

The first church, and one that I have already mentioned, was Reed Springs Baptist Church. I served as the youth pastor for five years, and it was an amazing ministry with wonderful people. It was during those years that I first had a lot of opportunities to lead in ministry, and it was also where my visionary leadership first became obvious.

The second church is Delano Baptist, and it is where I am serving today as the senior pastor. By the time I became the pastor there in 2018, I was very aware of the areas that I did well in. Also, I knew there were things that I continued to do that got me in trouble. The problem was, I really did not know how to fix those things.

In the four years that I have been there, God has used the people, and situations, to get me to a really good place in ministry. Not perfect, but much better than it was. You will see that all of those things were not good, nor were they easy. However, God still used them for my good (Romans 8:28).

If you are an individual who works with a visionary pastor, I pray that my story helps you guide your pastor. The book is easily divided. I use the first chapter to share how God led me to understand that I was a visionary pastor. After that, there are four parts. Part one is all about identifying and understanding a visionary pastor. You will see through my experience that these kinds of leaders think differently and do things differently. If you are to help your pastor, you need to understand him.

The second part is about how you can help and not hinder your visionary pastor. I discuss things that people have done, which was really a hindrance to me. It's not that they meant to, but it is just how it ended up. It may be the key to help you understand how you can encourage rather than hinder the man that God has led to be your pastor.

While part two is about the things that were more of a hindrance to me, part three is about the positives. In those chapters, I share with you the things that are happening which have helped me begin to lead as a visionary pastor. If you are going to help your visionary leader succeed, you need to know what not to do, and what to do. Parts two and three should give you some ideas.

The fourth and final part is somewhat of a culmination. It is all about where I am in the ministry, currently. God has brought me to the place where I know what kind of leader He has wired me to be, as well as the things I need to do to succeed. This section has to do with waiting on the Lord to do what only He can do.

You will see that visionary leaders need other people around them, who are gifted in different ways. They need these people to work alongside them, helping them, as well as challenging them, when need be. In this final section, I will show you how God finally got me to the place where I need to be. That place is where I have fully surrendered to Him, and He has supplied everything I need, in order for me to succeed as the pastor He has wired me to be.

For those of you who work with visionary pastors, I really do believe that my book can help. It will show you what to do, what not to do, and how to help your pastor learn to fully trust in the Lord, and the people He brings into your pastor's life and ministry. I pray that you will be the ally your leader needs, so that he can be the visionary that God created him to be.

Chapter One

My Personal Journey: Leading to Discovery

I am so thankful for strong, Christian roots. The Apostle Paul illustrated just how important they were, when writing to young Timothy, his son in the faith. In 2 Timothy 1:5, the Bible says, "For I am mindful of the sincere faith within you, which first dwelt in your grandmother Lois and your mother Eunice, and I am sure that *it is* in you as well." In the same letter, in 3:14-15, Paul went on to write, "You, however, continue in the things you have learned and become convinced of, knowing from whom you have learned *them*, and that from childhood you have known the sacred writings which are able to give you the wisdom that leads to salvation through faith which is in Christ Jesus" (NASB).

No doubt, the Scriptures that Timothy learned were taught to him by his Mama, and Mamaw (In my neck of the woods that's what you call your Mom and Grandmother). He was fortunate to have strong roots. I love what MacDonald said about the influence Timothy's mother had in verse 15. He wrote, "There is even the thought here that when his mother taught him his ABC's, she did so by using portions of the OT **Scriptures**." [1]

For many of us visionary pastors, we were blessed to be raised in churches, where the truth of our sins and its consequences, the good news of the Gospel, and Jesus being the only way to God, were faithfully taught in Sunday School classes, and from behind the pulpit. For that reason, I came to know Christ at the age of 7.

In those small, mountain, Baptist churches, I remember hearing about Jesus' death on the cross for our sins, the importance of baptism, as well as being faithful to the local church, and the need to be different from the world. What I do not remember hearing a lot about was the Great Commission, as it related to making disciples, and doing so beyond your own neighborhood or workplace. Those

---

[1] William MacDonald, *Believer's Bible Commentary*, (Nashville: Thomas Nelson Publishers), 1985, 2123.

things may have been taught, but they were not driven home as much as the other things.

Another thing I did not hear much about was how God has given us many different leadership styles. I never heard anything, in any church event, where different styles were described. I just thought all the leaders did the same things, the same ways. It was a few years into my ministry that God began to reveal some of that faulty thinking.

Much of my thought processes, in my early years in the church, came from some funny ideas. They are funny to me now, but I believed them back then. One of those ideas that many people in those churches had was that Seminary, or any kind of Bible College, would corrupt a preacher. I have actually had people tell me that. Not everyone believed that, but some did. I also heard that all of the educated preachers thought they were better than everyone else, and preached way above the average layman's ability to comprehend. Because of these things, I started out my ministry thinking this way.

A few years into my ministry, I was introduced to the preaching of Dr. Adrian Rogers and Dr. Charles Stanley. After listening to several of their sermons, I realized that my thinking was all wrong. These guys were not only educated, but they communicated in a way that anyone could understand them. They did not get away from the things that the Bible taught, as I had believed educated preachers did.

Shortly after being introduced to this preaching, I knew that education was the direction in which God was leading me. Before I knew it, I was enrolled as a college student at Liberty University, where I studied and earned my Bachelor's Degree in religion. This would be a major step toward me learning that God had gifted me a certain way. In many of the classes, I learned about how God uses people differently based on how they are wired. I feel like my Christian education really was the beginning of me learning what a visionary pastor was, and how to lead that way.

It was while I was a youth pastor at Reed Spring's that my visionary leadership style really surfaced. Even though I was learning about the different styles at Liberty, it would take years and tons of mistakes before it would really sink in. My years as a youth pastor was where most of those mistakes happened.

The youth group had great parents, who would go with their kids on many different mission endeavors, some of which you will read about. Even though they got frustrated with me, due to my lack of organization, they faithfully stood beside me. I am forever indebted to them for hanging in there, and never giving up on me.

It was during those years of ministry that the ball started rolling, and I would be in a process where I would eventually understand that God had created me to be a visionary leader, as well as what all that entailed. It was a slow process that lasted the entire five years that I was there. You can only imagine the roller coaster ride that this church and myself were on.

By the time I became the full-time pastor of Delano Baptist almost four years ago, I thought I had learned enough lessons from previous ministries to prevent me from getting us into the same kinds of unorganized situations. However, I guess I had not. Shortly after being there, my strong, visionary, leadership style began to rear its unorganized head. This time, when I reached that point, I handled things a little differently.

Though I had some understanding of my leadership skills before becoming the pastor at Delano, it was the first time I began to fully grasp that many of the problems I was encountering were as a result of my leadership style. I went to a few people at church, and I went to them many times. I began to pour my heart out about how I always seemed to lead the church in the same direction. I told them that at the beginning of all pastoral positions, it was all exciting. However, in a short time, the wheels always came off.

I am so thankful for the people that I went to. They sat down with me and helped me to realize that being a visionary was all that I had the ability to do, and there was nothing wrong with that (I had never had anyone put it the way they did). We talked about steps I needed to take, in order to get others involved with me in organizing the things God lays on my heart. After talking to them, I would start out the right way, and then fall off the wagon. Each time I did, they were there to reach out their hand and put me back on.

Besides pastoring, at this moment, I am also working on my Master of Divinity degree from Southeastern Baptist Theological Seminary. In my very first semester as a student there, I took a Christian Leadership Class, which was taught by one of America's military heroes. His name is Dr. Jeff Struecker. Dr. Struecker did a fantastic job of illustrating what it meant to be a visionary leader. God's timing is always perfect. Because I had been learning these things about myself through the ministry, the class just confirmed what I was thinking was true. I was a visionary pastor, and I needed to learn to lead that way. Through this class, as well as the people at my church, I feel God has brought me to a wonderful point in my ministry.

My early Christian roots are so important to me. I am thankful that I was taught about accepting Jesus as my Savior, and living for Him, as I supported the local church. If it wasn't for those faithful people teaching me, I would not be where I am. I also praise God for the things I have learned in other ways, which led me to getting my education, and learning how to lead churches into fulfilling the Great Commission, as well as Dr. Struecker's amazing class.

While I have made many mistakes along the way, God used a lot of people, and circumstances to get me where I am. It is because of Jesus, and His church that I am learning to be more of what He has called me to be. I am surrounded with people who have taught me what being a visionary is all about, and my church family continually reaches out their hands to pull me back on the wagon every time I fall off.

Section One
Identifying and Understanding a Visionary Pastor

Chapter Two

More and More; Bigger and Better with Unlimited Resources

All of us understand what it is like to desire a future, which is much better than what we are experiencing in the present. As I type from my home office, the date is July 19, 2020. We are in the middle of a year that has been, at best, challenging. For those of us living in the south, we may not even get football this year. That in and of itself is a crisis for many. We are all anticipating the time when the consequences of this Covid19 thing is in the rearview mirror.

Even in the Bible days, it was a common thing for people to look to the future in anticipation. Jesus' disciples were doing just that, right before the Son of God ascended into heaven. In Acts 1:6, the Bible says, "So when they had come together, they were asking Him, saying, "Lord, is it at this time You are restoring the kingdom to Israel?" (NASB). For Jesus' disciples, their entire focus was on the setting up of the Messiah's Kingdom. They were anticipating the day when they were no longer under the control of the Romans. [2]

For visionary pastors like myself, we are always looking at the future. I always tell people that when God puts a vision on my heart, it is in its future, perfect form. I can leave the church to go home and, by the time I get there, I have visualized a full-blown, world-wide ministry. When I pull into my driveway 15-20 minutes later, I would have visualized this ministry with hundreds of volunteers, working in three different countries, with unlimited resources. When these things come to mind, they are so awesome that I cannot help but believe that they are from God.

In my introduction, I mentioned the ministry we had started, which I thought was ready to go world-wide. At that time, I was serving at Reed Springs; it was the greatest church my family and I had served in up to that point. As crazy as I was, the students and parents

---

[2] John MacArthur, *The Bible Commentary* (Nashville: Thomas Nelson, 2005), 1432.

seemed to love us. They were willing to follow me pretty much anywhere, in order to do ministry.

This "world-wide" ministry that began in this church, started with a group of the students and their parents doing simple backyard Bible clubs in underprivileged apartment complexes. A few weeks after we started doing the ministry, I visualized it going bigger. My idea was that we build carnival games and take them into these places. I am not talking about little, simple games either. I wanted them to be much like what you would see at an amusement park, or county fair. I pushed my friend and ministry partner, Luke, into helping design and build them.

I felt that the games turned out great, and they looked wonderful. We started taking them and having Saturday block parties, and onsite VBS the weeks following the block parties. I was having the time of my life. I loved doing outreach more than anything else at that time, so everything was going really well. That is, until reality set in.

While the games looked awesome, and the kids seemed to enjoy them, they were a lot of work. It would take us over an hour just to get everything loaded up. When we arrived at the apartments, it took another hour and a half to get them set up. We were doing this ministry in the middle of the summer. If you have ever been to east Tennessee, you know that summers can be miserable. High temperatures, and high humidity. Luke was a trooper. I remember him doing most of the work because I was usually pulled in a lot of directions (my wife reminded me I was actually off talking). By the time everything started, he was soaking wet with sweat.

In my mind, I felt that if we were not successful in taking these games, we would have failed. I look at that now and realize it was not true, but I believed it then. After some time, the whole idea of loading and taking the games, setting them up, doing ministry, taking them down, loading them back up, and finally dropping them back off at the church, became too much. My wife started to complain and that bothered me. Later, parents (who were the volunteers that helped) asked me if we had to take the games. It felt as though we were being defeated.

The thing that really stressed me out was that I had put myself in a position where I had no choice but for this ministry to succeed, exactly as I had visualized it. I had contacted the Tennessee Baptist

Convention about doing a partnership with our ministry. The person I spoke with told me that the Convention was forming a partnership with the Baptist churches of Montana. She told me that there would be representatives from Montana coming to Nashville on a certain day. We set it up for me to go and speak with them.

My wife and I went to Nashville, and I met with a couple of the ladies who had come. I told them all about the ministry, and how we were doing block parties with big carnival games, and on-site VBS. I do not remember the exact conversation, but I must have sold that ministry. We got signed up to work with a church. Even though I meant well, we were not even close to being the ministry that I portrayed us to be, yet in my head, we definitely were.

After meeting with these ladies, I got into contact with the church that we would be working with. I told the pastor the same things I had told them in Nashville. He asked if we could come up, do the ministry, and build the same kinds of games that we had. Without even asking anyone, I told him that we could. I do not know what the people at my church thought when I told them what we would be doing, but I do know they must have loved me in spite of my issues. In a few months, we ended up going to Montana, doing the ministry, and building games for them.

This was not the end of the vision I had. After we finished in Montana, I wanted to go to another State, and help them. After that, another State. I had even discussed the idea of going to Brazil. I am so glad that I never got anywhere with any of the other States or Brazil. Can you see the problem? I wanted to go help the State of Montana, as well as any other State that would let us help them, yet we had not even figured out how to successfully do the ministry in the small town of about 500, where the church was located

The whole problem was I was always focused on the future. What was going on in the present was never enough. I wanted to do more and more and go bigger and better. For visionary pastors, this is a battle that we face in our minds. When God lays a vision on our hearts, we see the big picture. Getting there is the challenge.

After some time, I realized that the carnival game idea was not flying. It would have been successful if it had been thought out, and we had the resources that we needed. We never did get to that point. While I should have learned a ton of lessons from that situation, I would continue getting myself into those kinds of circumstances (though not all to that extreme) in all the other places that I served. While the vision that God lays on the pastor's hearts is important, it is also vital to take the right steps to get there.

Besides always being focused on the future, and how ministries can go bigger and better, there is another challenge that we visionaries face. That is, we do not really think about the resources that are needed. For me, I hardly ever think about money, or what is needed to make something happen. This was evident when we were planning the mission trip to Montana.

By the time I had contacted the pastor, after meeting with the ladies in Nashville, we only had a few months before we were leaving for the mission trip. We had over 30 people signed up, and I was excited and ready to go. Once I knew the costs for everyone to get an airplane ticket, as well as the hotel expense, I held a meeting with the group that was going.

I will never forget the night that we had the meeting. One of the men, David, which was going on the trip was a leader in our church, as well as a very successful businessman. He was the true definition of a servant. This man was always doing things to help needy people in the community, and this included doing a lot of things with his own money, which no one else knew he was doing. While I have the utmost respect for him, and feel that he walks close to the Lord, that night I was frustrated.

I began the meeting by letting all the parents and kids know what we would be doing on the trip. The pastor had set it up for us to go into three different parks that week and do children's ministry. We were going to use the later part of each day to build the games. After laying out the plan, I then discussed the airline information as well as hotel stay. It was at this point that things went in a direction I did not want them to go.

Once I finished, David asked me how much the trip was going to cost. I was young and not very smart at that time, and I always got frustrated over questions about costs. I remember saying something about how God can supply all that we need. He went on to say that he knew that, but raising the money was something that we would have to do. It was at this point that I told him we would need around $20,000.00. I said it as if it was $50.00. After all, God created this world, and He owns the cattle on a thousand hills (Psalm 50:10), $20,000.00 to Him is nothing. That was what was going on in my head at that moment.

I thought he was going to fall out of his chair when I told him. Because of me, not him, things got somewhat tense. I just had this crazy idea that we should never worry about money or resources because God can give us what we need. Now that I am older, I would like to go back in time and slap the younger me upside the head for some of the stupid stuff that I said. Yes, God owns it all. In Psalm 24:1, it says, "The earth is the Lord's, and all it contains, The world, and those who dwell in it." (NASB). That verse, however, does not give us an excuse to be stupid.

When my wife and I left the meeting, she set me straight. She told me that "just because Jamie Johnson walks around with no worries in the world, does not mean that he should expect everybody else to think like him!" She went on to tell me that the church needed people who thought about those things, or it would end up going broke. Now that I look back on it, I realize that David was doing what he was supposed to do. As a man who owned his business, thinking about money was something that he had to do.

I have thought about that night many times. David is a man who lives by faith on a daily basis. I have witnessed this on many occasions. The problem was, I was living in this imaginary world where you just lay out the vision, do not even worry about the resources, and trust God. However, after being in the ministry for 22 years, I now understand that things take time. God is an awesome God, who gives pastors great visions. However, those visions often take a long time to bring to fruition, and resources are sometimes hard to acquire. God provides, but it may not happen when we want it to, or how. In the end the goal is for God to get the glory.

One of the characteristics of visionary leaders is their intense focus on the future. They are always trying to get to the big picture and get there quickly. If they are like me, they do not automatically think about what it takes to get there, money or any other resource. While it is exciting to see what God can do when the vision is completed, there is a lot of struggle for those who do not know how to take the necessary steps. You may be the one to help your pastor create those small steps that will lead to the fulfillment of his God-given vision.

Chapter Three

That Sounds Awesome! But Where is the Organization?

I have always loved the story of Nehemiah, in the Old Testament. To me, he was one of the great visionary leaders of all time. The thing that impresses me most is that he not only was able to visualize, but the Old Testament brother could organize. A skill that many of us visionary pastors lack.

Even though I have preached sermons on Nehemiah many times, it wasn't until recently that I thought about his ability to visualize and organize. After God worked it out for him to go before the king and get permission to return to Jerusalem, he had the opportunity to gather all the resources he needed, in order to rebuild the walls.

Once he got back home, it was Nehemiah himself (not someone he delegated) who, at night, surveyed the walls (Neh. 2:12-15). He then went on to let the other leaders know what his assessment was. After that, Nehemiah put together a work force to start the job.[3] He was a highly gifted visionary leader, who also had the ability to organize. Eventually, Nehemiah and his team of workers were able to fight through opposition, and discouragement, until they saw the vision that he had, completely fulfilled.

For many of us visionaries, we could not even organize a picnic with three people, much less put together a team of individuals, assess the entire situation, and organize it so that the goal is accomplished. In a ton of situations I have had people tell me, "This is so unorganized!" The things that were unorganized, were always the things I had put together. Through some situations that happened to me, which I will describe, you will see that this is a battle that I continually deal with.

When I first met with the pulpit committee at Delano about taking my first full-time ministry position, I shared with them my desire to

---

[3] Youngblood, Bruce, and Harrison eds., *Nelson's New Illustrated Bible Dictionary* (Thomas Nelson: Nashville, 1995), 889.

lead the church into fulfilling the Great Commission. Because it was a church full of working people, they seemed to really dig that. It made me super excited because I knew that being full-time would afford me the opportunity to get even more ministry done. While that was true, it was also a recipe for disaster in light of my visionary mind.

As soon as I became the new pastor of Delano Baptist, I did what I have always done, I started really fast. During my first meeting with the pulpit committee, the members told me that the church had a lot of people who loved to do ministry. In my mind, that meant the sky was the limit. I began meeting with people and telling them all about the things I had visualized for us to do. And after about a year and a half, I did it again. I got us into a disorganized mess.

After pushing to start all kinds of new ministries, I ran into a couple of circumstances, which made me realize something. We had 5 or 6 ministries which had begun, but only one of them was actually off the ground and moving. This ministry that had really taken off was the clothes closet.

The idea for this ministry began at Pat and Nat's home. Pat serves as Delano's outreach director, and a deacon. The idea for the ministry started, as we were brainstorming about different kinds of ministry that would fly at the church. From there, it sold well to the congregation, and we had a woman, Becky, who was willing to lead that ministry. A few months later, Darla joined her as the assistant. These ladies are energetic and hard-working. They dug their heels in this ministry and it was off and running.

Once I realized that we had all of these ministries, yet the clothes closet was the only one that was running with a lot of success, I sought advice from one of our deacons. After seeking guidance from Steve, and getting his answer, I knew what had to be done. We needed to focus on the ministries that were doing well, and hold off on the others, until we could run them effectively.

Even though I thought I had it all figured out, I was wrong again. Shortly after I zoned in on the clothes closet, and abandoned things that were not working, we started realizing some things. We hosted the clothes closet ministry one Saturday morning per month. Everything was very organized, and seemed to flow well, but there was a problem. Because we did not really put a lot of restrictions on what people could take, some individuals from the community started taking advantage of us.

There were people who were taking bags of clothes every month. These people were getting more clothes in one day than I have bought in years. Also, it was during this time that we had a local food bank. Just like our ministry, people could come and get food one day per month. While helping with the food bank, something hit me.

A lot of the same people, who were coming to the food bank, also came to our clothes closet. These were individuals who did not have a job (but a lot of them seemed healthy enough to work) and were drawing a check each month. The food bank was in the afternoon, and some of these people were wearing pajamas when they came to get their "groceries." The sad part was that in the back of the car were their kids: young children, pre-teens, and teenagers. This was a terrible example the parents were setting for the people of the future. With our eyes solely focused on the clothes closet, what could we do?

The last thing we needed to do was take a situation that needed some organization and add more ministry to it. But, guess what? That's exactly what I did. My vision was to make the clothes closet a one-stop-shop. An attainable goal (at least in my mind) would be to create plans for these individuals, so that they could realize there was an opportunity for a better future, than to just draw a government check each month. If nothing else, we should try to help their kids understand the need to break this cycle.

This is where I really dug myself, and our directors, in a hole. With good intentions, I started reaching out to services within the community that helped these individuals. I told them all about what I was thinking, and how our church wanted to get them out of the situation they were in. Before I knew it, I was getting phone calls by these organizations, asking if our church could pay people's electric bills. I know that these organizations thought that was the kind of thing we wanted to do but, in reality, paying their bills really never helped them.

At this time, I was also calling Becky with all of these ideas, plus more (which I do not have time to describe) and I told her that I had been contacting people, and we really needed to help these individuals get out of the situations that they had gotten themselves into. Becky was gracious but seemed a bit quiet about my ideas. One night, I understood why.

One Wednesday evening, we had a meeting with all the heads of the departments and committees. Before the meeting, Pat told me something that I was unaware of. He said that if we were not careful, Becky and Darla were going to burn out. There were some things that Becky had been doing that were just too much for one individual. Once Becky came into the meeting, and explained what was going on, I got it.

Becky told us that every day, when she got home from work, she came to the church until late in the evening. People had been leaving bags of clothes on the front porch of the church. Also, others were just laying bags in various places inside the church. We had so many clothes donated each week, that we were running out of room to store them. Becky also came out every Saturday, with a small group of people, in order to organize. Still, it did not get completed.

As she was talking, I realized that Becky was not getting a break. She said it felt like she was drowning. I am not the smartest guy in the world, but I realize one thing. When you are a pastor, and one of your dedicated workers tells you that ministry is making her feel like she's drowning, something had better change.

During that meeting, it occurred to me. We had a ministry that needed organization, and it needed it yesterday. Instead of creating more stuff to do, it was necessary that we pause, and get things fixed. I was trying to add things that would make it worse, rather than better. That night, a plan was put together. That plan's success depended on me getting out of people's way, letting them do their job, and to quit trying to develop more new ministries before we were ready.

Nat came up with some ideas about how things could be organized. Immediately, she started putting things into place that made it successful. They also were able to get more people from the church to come out and help throughout the week. We made sure that Becky quit coming on weeknights, and that she could clear her head and I got completely out of the way.

Once all of this happened, I had a talk with Mindy. I told her that I just did not get it. It seemed that when I would cast my visions that people really bought in. Early on, people would sign up with whatever I wanted to do. At the end of the day, I would be standing there with an unorganized mess. Mindy said something that has helped me understand. She said, "Jamie, people get excited because you are so full of energy, and they love seeing you like this, and some people do not want to make you feel disappointed."

A couple of weeks ago, at the small-group meeting at Pat and Nat's, something else was said that brought clarity to me. We got on the subject of me being such a strong visionary. I wanted to get everyone's insight on why these things always happen, and what needed to be done. So, I gave them an example of what I had been visualizing lately.

Because of the COVID 19 situation, I have had more time at home, which has given me the opportunity to come up with all kinds of stuff. Lately, I have been focused on the kinds of ministry we can do when the church is back up and running strong. As usual, the things I have visualized would probably take years to get accomplished but, because of how I think, it feels that we should be able to get it done immediately.

When laying out this plan at Pat and Nat's, I told everyone how my mind worked, when it came to the visions that I had. I explained to them that, according to my thinking, we should just be able to take these things and begin to implement them. However, I also knew that this was not reality. I told them that that was the battle I faced, daily.

Just like Mindy, Becky gave great advice. She said that people get excited because my visions do seem awesome, and something that people want to do. The problem is I need other individuals to help lay out the steps it takes to get there. Unfortunately, getting there may take much longer than I would like for it to. But, if I let it happen as it's supposed to, it will be way more effective. Visualizing is great, but there has to be organization to it, or it won't last.

All of this takes me to something the Apostle Paul wrote. In Ephesians 4:11-13, the Bible says,

> *And He gave some as apostles, and some as prophets, and some as evangelists, and some as pastors and teachers, for the equipping of the saints for the work of service, to the building up of the body of Christ; until we all*

> *attain to the unity of the faith, and of the knowledge of the Son of God, to a mature man, to the measure of the stature which belongs to the fullness of Christ* (NASB).

Paul, under the inspiration of the Holy Spirit, is telling Christians that God gives believers gifts and equips them to use those gifts. It is God who chooses which gifts and abilities we are to have. Besides those gifts, He also has given leaders the ability to lead in certain ways.

For people like me, as well as the leader God has called to your church, He has called us to be not only pastors, but visionary pastors. I know there are some who have the same gifts that Nehemiah had, but many of us visionaries just do not have organizational skills embedded in us. This is a hard lesson I am learning every day.

In some of the places that I have served, when I would cast the vision, people felt that I had the ability to organize it. After some time, we ended up in situations similar to the one I described concerning the clothes closet. It was at that time that I began to lose people on what I was trying to do. We ended up starting ministries and, before they could succeed, I had already given up on them and began something new. Always doing this is a good indication that you can visualize, but not organize.

When I first began to realize that I was weak in the area of organization, I thought I should just keep chipping away at being an organizer. Even though I tried, I could just never get it. The truth is, sometimes God just does not equip you to do certain things. Some may work at it, and learn to organize but, for me, that was not the case. That is what happened with our clothes closet. I do feel that my organizational skills are a little better, but not great. No matter how hard I try, I am a visualizer, not an organizer.

The moment Steve gave me the advice about making some ministries inactive, I thought I was good. Even when I focused on the clothes closet, and tried to add more ministries to it, it felt like I was becoming more organized. The truth was, just because I had my mind on one ministry, did not mean that ministry was organized. Trying to add more stuff on, at a time when what we were doing was not working, was not organization, at all. It is just adding unorganized chaos to a situation that was already lacking in structure.

If your pastor seems to always end up in this same kind of mess, keep in mind, that is not what he intends on doing. He is very excited about the things that he feels God has laid on his heart, he just does not have the skills to organize it. If he is like me, he may be learning the hard way that his visions may take longer than he wants them to. Stand behind him, encourage him concerning his excitement, but lovingly help him understand that taking the right steps of organization is just as important as pursuing the dream that God has given him.

Chapter Four
Don't Throw Out the Baby with the Bathwater

Throughout my entire childhood, and for most of my adult life, I had low self-esteem. I was an awkward looking kid. I had big feet, big ears, long thick legs, and a very skinny upper body. I not only looked awkward, but I felt every bit of it.

To say my childhood was not great would be a huge understatement. I always felt the need to try to fit in and be one of the "cool kids." Growing up in the era that I did, my favorite television personality was "The Fonz," from the show "Happy Days." Just as much as Arthur Fonzarelli was cool, I wanted to be just as cool. Unfortunately, I never felt like I got to that point.

Besides my awkwardness, things happened when I was a kid, which helped contribute to my self-esteem being pretty much destroyed. For this book, I will not get into it. This carried on into my adulthood. For that reason, when I was constructively criticized as an adult, it would shut me down. Many times I have gone into an almost depressed state as a result. I told myself that I would never be able to get anywhere, and it made it difficult for me to take any chances. When I did, I often had anxiety attacks over it. This kept me from having the confidence that I needed, in order to do anything that was overly challenging for me.

The biggest breakthrough I had, which helped me get past this thought process, did not even happen at church, or as a result of church leaders. It happened in a factory. It was during a time when I was a bi-vocational pastor, and my production line was working every weekend. In order for me to be off on Sundays, I had to get people to work for me. I began praying that God would open a door for me to be off on weekends. He did more than that!!!

God worked it out, by using a very good friend and former boss of mine, Jim. Because of him, I received a promotion, and started working in a salaried position. This job was a white-collar job, but I also had the opportunity to help the people on the production lines, where I had worked for 10 years. It was a win/win situation for me.

Within our department, people in my position were Kaizen Specialists. There were also Kaizen Technicians in the same department, who had the job of building things that made the production lines run better. It required them to be mechanically inclined. I never felt like I was a mechanical person, so I did not even attempt to try to do anything that required the use of mechanical skills.

Within this department, we interacted with the technicians every day. When someone from the production lines that we supported needed something built, our techs asked us to get drawings, or prints. All of that was a bit challenging for me. Each time I went to those guys with something, I just knew I would be exposed because of my ignorance.

Soon after working in this department, there were a couple of guys, Danny and Marcus, who treated me much differently than I expected. They would ask me to go to the lines with them, and they would show me how to do things. Reluctantly, I went. Not because of them, but because of all the lies I told myself.

I remember letting those guys know that I had never learned how to do some of the stuff they were showing me, and they were extremely kind. They reassured me that if I had never learned it, there would be no reason for me to think that I should just be able to do it. They said they would teach me. They really helped me learn to relax and not worry about making mistakes in front of people. After a while, they had me doing things that I thought I could never do. Even when I did mess something up, they never went back and made fun of me for it.

Even though the things they taught me were such a benefit to re-building self-esteem, it was what they continually said that has stuck with me and helped me as a pastor. I can hear Marcus now, "All of us have different skill sets. It's not that anyone is better than the other." Danny would say the same kinds of things. These guys knew that even though they could teach me how to do a lot of things, there were just some things that I would never be great at, and vice versa.

The reason why this aspect of my life is so important is because it has positively affected how I view myself within ministry. For so many years, when I would hear comments about how I could not organize, I felt defeated. The devil, whom the Bible says, "is like a roaring lion seeking whom he may devour" (1 Peter 5:8) would begin to whisper in my ear. It was not an audible voice, but it was loud enough to create chaos within my spirit. "Just quit. You will never be able to do anything right." All of this only because people said that I could not organize.

One of the amazing things about God's Word is that it cancels out Satan's lies, with God's truth. Satan is telling pastors all kinds of things, in order to try to get them to throw in the towel. For many visionary pastors, he is telling them that because their disorganization keeps putting them in bad situations, they need to give up. They will never get where they need to be. The Word of God says differently.

One of my favorite verses is Jeremiah 1:5. "Before I formed you in the womb I knew you; Before you were born I sanctified you; I ordained you a prophet to the nations" (NASB). This prophet had a difficult ministry ahead of him, and the people he preached to would never listen. He would have great and promising prophecies to the southern kingdom of Judah, which would be fulfilled, but those things would happen well after his ministry. Nevertheless, the great thing about Jeremiah's ministry was that God had ordained and sanctified Him to do what He called Him to do, regardless of how things looked at the time.

When God calls pastors into the ministry, He has already ordained and sanctified them. They are equipped to do what God has called them to do, regardless of what skills they are lacking. The key for them is to learn to utilize the skills He has given them, and to surround themselves with people who are strong, in the areas where they are weak.

In Psalm 131:14, the Bible says, "I will give thanks to You, for I am fearfully and wonderfully made; Wonderful are Your works, And my soul knows it very well" (NASB). This verse alone tells us that God gave each leader the abilities that he has. For whatever the reason, he was not created to be strong in some areas. It is important to learn to celebrate the skill sets that God has given your pastor, rather than staying focused on the things he is not great at.

Think about this, even within the Bible, people were different. I have a red-headed friend, Jason, who said his favorite disciple was Peter. Jason and I worked together over 20 years ago and we would often discuss Scripture. One day when talking about Peter, we both decided that this dude must be red-headed. When Jesus was in the Garden of Gethsemane, they came to arrest Him, Peter cut off one of Malchus' ears (John 18:10). Who does that? A red-head with a fiery temper.

In reality, with Peter being a Jew, I seriously doubt he had red-hair. He did, however, have a strong personality. There he was, fighting for his Savior. He was also the disciple who was the first to speak up. When reading the Gospels, you will find, none of the other disciples were like him, nor was he like those guys. People were all created with a different personality.

Going all the way back to Genesis 10:8-9, the Bible says, "Now Cush became the father of Nimrod; he became a mighty one on the earth. He was a mighty hunter before the Lord; therefore it is said, "Like Nimrod a mighty hunter before the Lord'" (NASB). We all know the stories of Peter. But, who is this Nimrod character? While there is way less information about him, we know that he had a skill that not everyone had. He was not just a hunter, but a mighty hunter.

As a visionary leader, your pastor's focus needs to be on what God made him good at. Just because he is not great at some things, does not mean that he is holding God hostage. Like Peter, he has a specific personality. Also, like Nimrod, he has a skillset. Let me use my imagination for a moment. Think of it like this, if Nimrod were living today, we might say something like this. "That dude can shoot a deer from 400 yards away, without ever missing the exact part of the deer he is aiming at, but he ain't strong enough to drag the thing out of the woods. That's what his friends are for."

It does not matter how good of a hunter he is, if that deer does not make it to the back of his truck, it will never end up in your chili. Do not throw the baby out with the bath water. Sure there are some areas that your pastor will always struggle in, but it does not negate the ones where he excels. As someone who comes alongside him, always remind him that he was fearfully, and wonderfully made.

Even though there are some areas where he is not strong, and needs people to help him, celebrate the good things, rather than always harping on the bad.

Section Two
Helping, and Not Hindering the Visionary Pastor

Chapter Five

You Keep Popping My Balloon

There is no doubt in my mind, whatsoever, that I have been blessed with the most amazing wife in the entire world. When we got married on January 20, 1996, she was not a Christian, and I was not living for Christ as I should. In February of 1998, she got saved, and both of us started serving the Lord.

In July of the same year, God called me to preach the Gospel, and I have tried to be faithful in doing so ever since. When I first recognized that He may be calling me, I asked my wife something. "If I start preaching, will you stay with me?" "Of course!" were the words that my wife answered with. Not only has she stayed with me, but she has stood beside me in every decision I have made, good or bad.

Even though she has never left my side, Mindy and I have not always agreed on things I wanted to do in the ministry. Much of this has to do with our extreme differences in personalities. For anyone who has spent 5 minutes with me, they realize that I have never been in any kind of shell. I am probably the most extroverted person they have ever met. Plus, I have a booming outside voice, and I am terrible at trying to use my "inside voice."

My sweet wife is way more introverted, and she doesn't like attention brought to her. Mindy could go out and literally save the entire world from a catastrophe, and she would ask me to be the one to go on the news and explain what happened. She doesn't care about accolades. She always wants to be behind the scenes.

All of us have been in Walmart and heard the loud, obnoxious dude who seems to want everyone to listen to him. Apparently, I'm that dude, or so I've been told. There have been many times when we were walking through a store that Mindy has asked me to be quiet. It's not that I want people to listen to me, it's just that I naturally talk loudly, and I'm just not overly concerned about what strangers think about me. She would go on to say that people were staring at me. To which I would reply, "I don't care if they are looking at me!" I've learned to come down off of that attitude a bit, realizing how it affects her, and that it is pretty rude of me.

Another big difference between my wife and me is that I am a huge risk taker, when I feel that God is leading me in a certain direction. As I mentioned earlier, I have had low self-esteem when it came to taking certain risks involving things that were more secular, so I would avoid them. However, when it comes to ministry related things, being a risk taker is one of my main characteristics. If I felt confident that God was in something, I was always ready to jump in headfirst.

One example of this happened when I knew God was leading me to step away from bi-vocational ministry and take on a full-time role. I just knew that God was going to open that door, and I expected it to happen very soon. One day, during this particular time in my ministry, I met Mindy for lunch. While we were eating, I overheard a group of people talking, and it became clear that they were part of a pulpit committee. This could possibly be God testing my faith.

I told my wife what they were saying, and I thought I should go introduce myself. That look on her face told me I had better not. I am also the guy who, when I overhear a conversation about things that interest me, I am tempted to jump in and talk to you about it. Apparently, to some people that is considered weird. Due to good judgment, I avoided introducing myself to that committee.

I have told my wife on many occasions, "You keep popping my balloon." I have felt like I am walking around with my pretty helium balloon on a string, and someone just walks by with a needle and pops it. It has always happened when I have told her about the ministry ideas that I have had.

I usually approach my wife first with the things that are going on in my mind. I was always waiting for her to stop in her tracks, place her hand over her heart, and say, "That is the most amazing ministry idea I have ever heard, Let's get this thing started!" You won't believe this, but that is not what she says.

My wife normally begins to say things like, "When do you plan on doing that? Jamie, you got too many irons in the fire right now. Who all are you calling, and how are you finding time to get the stuff done that you are supposed to do? Are you sure this is what you're supposed to be doing?" She always brought up these things because I would tell her that I had been on the phone with this person, or that person, as well as how many trips I had made to all the places that I had gone, trying to get this vision going.

I would always get so frustrated with her. I thought my wife was supposed to support all the visions that God put on my heart. Why does she keep on popping my balloon? I have finally realized that she was not tearing down my visions or saying they could not happen. It comes down to this, my wife is way more of an organizer, than a visionary.

Since 2010, Mindy has taught 2nd grade. She has explained to me that, if she plans a field trip, before the day it happens, she has to have all of her ducks in a row. She cannot just say, "Hey parents, we are taking a trip next Monday, have your kids here and ready to go." The parents will need way more information than that. While my visions look beautiful to me, and well put-together, there are no steps in getting us to the point of completion, like there are when she puts together a field trip. To me, it always felt as though I was laying out an awesome vision, with great structure. To the organized person, it might be a great vision, but there are no steps that will get us there.

My poor wife. She heard vision after vision by me. Each time, she tried to let me know that it would be hard to do what I wanted. She had watched me struggle and try to start things, just to watch them be abandoned before we got anywhere. The problem was, when she tried to give me advice, I would shut her out. When I wanted something to happen, I was very passionate, and felt that I had to make it work.

For some time now, I have learned to respect my wife's viewpoint way more than I did early on. She understands how I think now, so she works at helping me organize and think through things. Many of the leaders in my church have come alongside me to help as well. It was when they realized what was going on with me and reached out to me, that I began to understand that my wife was not someone holding a needle, just waiting to pop my balloon.

Jesus would say things sometimes, that probably felt like He was popping someone's balloon. I am reminded of a question brought to Jesus by James and John's mother, as well as how He answered it. In Matthew 20:20-23, the Bible says,

> *Then the mother of the sons of Zebedee came to Jesus with her sons, bowing down and making a request of Him. And He said to her, "What do you wish?" She said to Him, "Command that in Your kingdom these two sons of mine may sit one on Your right and one on Your left." But Jesus answered, "You do not know what you are asking. Are you able to drink the cup that I am about to drink?" They said to Him, "We are able." He said to them, 'My cup you shall drink; but to sit on My right and on My left, this is not Mine to give, but it is for those for whom it has been prepared by My Father.'"*

In putting yourself in this woman's shoes, don't you think she felt let down? She really had this dream of her babies seated in very important places in the Kingdom. We know that Jesus was not out to just destroy people's dreams, He was about telling them the truth.

For many years, people would either tag along with me, until they realized something wasn't working, or they would just be negative about the visions I presented. At Delano, I have had people handle things much differently. Instead of just being negative, they would say things like this, "Jamie, I love your vision, but let me help you organize it. I want it to be successful."

The people who told me this have not been visionaries. They were organizers, who made up their minds that they were going to help, and not hinder me. It was their approach that made all the difference. Yes, they were saying that the plan would not work the way I presented it, but not because of the kind of vision it was. These people stressed their desire to help me succeed, by making sure that it had the right structure.

We have all met people who are very negative. Their approach is much different. Every time you tell them anything, they have something bad to say about it, but they never discuss the good in what you have told them. That is the feeling visionary pastors get, when people seem to keep shooting down the ideas that they have.

Your visionary pastor may not show it, but I guarantee you that he gets very frustrated when people seem to just be negative about what he wants to do. It's as if he feels that he can conquer the world. He gets so excited and cannot wait to tell you about it. As soon as he tells you his vision, he hears the words, "That ain't going to work, or I don't think we have the money or enough help." I have heard those words many times, and it was difficult every time.

The first sermon I ever preached was on July 19, 1998. The passage was Exodus 17:12-14, the story of Moses, Aaron, and Hur. Israel was in a battle with one of their enemies, the Amalekites. During the battle, as long as Moses' hands were in the air, Israel prevailed. When they came down, they did not. Aaron and Hur teamed up. They gave Moses a rock to sit on, and they held his arms in the air until the sun went down, guaranteeing Israel the victory.

Visionary pastors need some men like Aaron and Hur. When they present the vision, but do not have the ability to put it all together, they can have people hold up their hands, and claim the victory of God's visions coming to fruition, as a result of the body working together as God intended it to. When your pastor shares his vision, rather than focusing on what will not work, help him think through everything. Don't pop his balloon, just help him realize the organized steps needed to ensure that his visions are a success.

Chapter Six

Don't Complain; Just Give Me a Solution

Even though all of us have a tendency to complain, those people who have the "spiritual gift" of complaining, well, they are a special kind of individual. As a pastor, those are often the ones I have the most trouble dealing with. There are people who complain about the music in the church. Some church members do not like more contemporary music, while others would gladly do away with the hymn books. There are people who complain about things like the temperature in the church, or the color of the walls, or where the piano sits. Believe it or not, I have dealt with the piano thing before.

When you have been in the ministry as long as I have been, you find that people will complain about the pastor. Sometimes it is warranted, and other times it is just because the ones complaining are really the problem. For me, I have no problem with people complaining, as long as they have a solution for what they are complaining about.

President, Teddy Roosevelt once said, "Complaining about a problem without proposing a solution is called whining" [4] I completely agree. Several years ago, when I was serving as a youth pastor, the senior pastor had me preach on a Wednesday night. I still remember that my sermon had something to do with being willing to forgive people.

After the service, I was approached by a woman in our church. She asked if she could talk to me. What she said to me, I have never had anyone say to me before that, or after. She said, "Jamie, last week, I ran your name in the ground. I talked bad about you to some people. I still don't like some of the things that you do, but I guess I have to get your forgiveness because that is what the Bible says for me to do"

---

[4] Theodore Roosevelt Quotes, *Goodreads*, https://www.goodreads.com/quotes/8011953-complaining-about-a-problem-without-posing-a-solution-is-called, accessed February 8, 2022.

At first I was thrown off. What in the world do you say to something like that? I realized that although she told me she was apologizing, that was not really an apology. I did not appreciate her approach, so I asked her a question. "These things you say that I do, do any of them have to do with me violating God's Word?" This woman went on to say that that was between me and God. Wrong answer.

The situation did not get any better. I went on to tell her that it was her responsibility to let me know what I had done wrong. If I had, in fact, done something offensive, I needed to know, so I could make it right. She never told me what it was. I came to the conclusion that she just did not like me, and that was her problem to deal with.

This is nothing compared to what some pastors go through on a daily basis. I have heard about pastors who get ugly notes written about them and left in the offering plate. It reminds me of a story about D.L. Moody. He was preaching one night, and someone wrote something on a piece of paper. Moody read it, and it said, "idiot." Moody, with all of his wit, said this, "I have received many letters where someone did not sign their name. This is the first time they signed their name, and didn't write the letter" [5]

Even though no one else has ever jumped me the same way that woman did, I have heard complaints that centered around the same thing. I have a tendency to fly by the seat of my pants. This is one of the characteristics of a pastor who is a visionary like myself. It's all because I am always looking at the big picture and do not think about the small details.

For many years, this flying by the seat of my pants thing got me in trouble. Believe it or not, one of the things people complained about was how I made announcements on Sundays. Not really something major. To be honest, if I never have to make another announcement on Sunday, I will be happy. My mind is always on what I am preaching, so talking about other events can be a disaster.

When it first got back to me that people did not like how I did it, I thought it was petty. However, after it was explained to me, I understood. In my mind, when we decide to do something, such as take our senior adults out for breakfast somewhere, this is all I need

---

5 D.L. Moody, The "Fool" says there is no God, Family Ties, https://www.family-times.net/illustration/Fool/201454/, accessed February 9, 2022

to say, "For all seniors going this Saturday, be here at 7am." For those of us who fly by the seat of our pants, no problem. For everyone else, that is kind of an issue.

I was told that people needed to know where we were going, what time we would be coming home etc. With something this minor, imagine my announcements concerning the bigger things. Unfortunately, my announcements for the big things were no different than the smaller.

I have been in other meetings where people would complain about how I did things. It always centered on the fact that they may have been great ideas, but they were never planned very well. Rather than jumping in, and saying, "Let me help you plan this." I often heard over and over about how bad my planning was. People did not realize it, but those kinds of things do not help a visionary minded pastor.

The reality is these pastors do not attempt to be weak in planning. If your pastor is like me, he has tried many times to make sure that things were planned out, and that he had an answer to every question someone may bring up. As much as I have attempted to be good at organization, things rarely worked like they should, if no one helped me plan.

One example happened when I was at Reed Springs. Our daughter, Abby, was a few months old. There was a particular town, which was known for its level of poverty. I had spoken to the local Baptist association in that town about bringing the youth group up there on a Saturday. Our mission, to hand out school supplies.

I have always been taught that the best way to organize something was to think about any question someone may bring up. When I spoke to the Director of Missions, Albert, I asked him about hotels. To which, he said, "Ya'll don't need to stay in a hotel, we got a real nice Christian camp up here you can stay in." I knew that the mothers who were coming with me would want to know what we needed to bring. I asked him. He said, "Just bring yourselves, we got everything you will need, everything!" He even asked me if my family was coming, and I told him they were. "We got a real nice family cabin for you, your wife, and kids to stay in."

After church the Wednesday before we left, I got nailed with questions. "Do we need to take blankets, towels, wash clothes, or anything else?" I told them "no." I explained that we would be staying in a super nice Christian camp. I remember making it sound like this place was high-end.

We went up to this camp, and things did not turn out like I had hoped. My baby girl was not happy at all. Mindy did not want to bring her in the first place, and I talked her into it. When we arrived, Abby was crying her eyes out. As Albert opened the cabins, the parents started going through all of them. All of a sudden, during a time when Abby was screaming bloody murder, I get flooded with questions.

"Where are the sheets and blankets, towels, wash cloths, soap, shampoo?" It went on and on. I asked and was told that they didn't have any of those things. A few minutes later, Mindy asked me where the nice cabin was that my family was staying in. I pointed it out, and she said what no man wants to hear, "Come here!" When we got to the cabin, my wife told me to go in, and walk to the back. When I did, the entire cabin tilted (I am not exaggerating). I realized then; my organization of this thing was not going as well as I had hoped. My thought, "If we can just get through the night, it will be all good tomorrow. We get to meet people's needs in the name of Jesus."

After managing to make it through the night, we headed to the church where we would be working. It was arranged for us to hand out the school supplies from the parking lot. We got there and the first thing we did was set up tables outside and put all the school supplies on them. We were instructed on how much to give each person. We had all the stuff on the tables, and now we were ready for people to come.

I don't remember why, but everyone had gone into the fellowship hall, and no one was outside. I went in to get them so we could be outside when people showed up. I walked in and, as usual, got sidetracked. After a few minutes we all went outside, and every school supply we had was gone! Someone drove up, loaded their car with everything, and took off.

Every time I think of that weekend, I am reminded of something. No matter how good I think I have gotten at not flying by the seat of my pants, and being good at organizing, I realize I will just never be great at it. For many years, people would just complain about what I did, but they never gave me any solutions. Complaining, without giving solutions, will never help anyone.

The Apostle Paul wrote letters to a church that was dealing with a lot of problems, the Corinthians. In 1 Corinthians 1:10-17, after talking about defilement within the congregation, he went on by describing a problem they were having with division. [6] What if he never gave them any solutions to their problems? It would never have helped them. The Apostle Paul did not work that way. When he told you that you had problems, he also shared ways that those problems could be solved.

I know it can get frustrating when your pastor tries to do things, and there is not much organization, but remember something. Your pastor is not intentionally doing what he does. He's leading the best way that he can. Even though he does not do well at putting the right steps together, be thankful that you have a pastor who has a vision to advance the Kingdom. Some pastors do not seem to have much concern about doing anything. Rather than just complaining, ask, "What do I need to do to help?" Be to your pastor what the Apostle Paul was to the people at the Church of Corinth. If you plan on complaining, help search for solutions.

---

[6] Warren W. Wiersbe, *The Bible Exposition Commentary: New Testament Volume 1 Matthew-Galatians*, (Colorado Springs: David C. Cook, 1989), 569.

Chapter Seven

Feel Free to Criticize, but Please be Constructive

All pastors understand how hard it is on them when it feels that people are popping their balloon, or complaining about how they lead, without offering a solution. It begins to feel personal, as if people are being critical of them as an individual. It is not that they want to feel this way, it is just how we have the tendency to let it affect us.

As an avid Tennessee Volunteer football fan, I have watched a lot of Southeastern Conference games, not only the ones where Tennessee is playing. Although I love my Vols, one must at least appreciate what Nick Saban has done at the University of Alabama. When watching games, I have heard something that many people say who have worked with him. It goes something to the effect of, "When you work with coach Saban, you have to remember, you cannot take it personally." It becomes clear what they mean when you see him in the face of assistant coaches and screaming at them on Saturdays. For us pastors, it would be good if we could learn the same thing. When people say negative things about how pastors lead, or the way they do certain things, it is important that they do not take it personally. The problem is our enemy is constantly trying to discourage pastors and drive them into giving up.

Concerning how all believers are to deal with spiritual warfare, in Ephesians 6:11-13, the Apostle Paul wrote, "Put on the full armor of God, so that you will be able to stand firm against the schemes of the devil. For our struggle is not against flesh and blood, but against the rulers, against the powers, against the world forces of this darkness, against the spiritual *forces* of wickedness in the heavenly *places*. Therefore, take up the full armor of God, so that you will be able to resist in the evil day, and having done everything, to stand firm" (NASB).

There are a couple of things that you may need to help your pastor understand, when feeling like people are being critical of him, personally. First, Paul is telling these leaders that their battle is not with other people. The person who is complaining about how unorganized they always seem to be, or how they never finish the things they started, those people are not their enemy. Their enemy is the devil.

Secondly, the times that your pastor gets down because things seem personal, those are the times that Satan is using his schemes to try to get him to give up. Because he has been gloriously saved, Satan cannot touch his salvation. He has to try to defeat him somehow, and he will definitely use what feels like criticism against him, in order to get him to give up. It just seems that the critical people are the enemy when that happens. I have been there many times.

For a number of years, I was not good with criticism at all. It did not matter whether the person was trying to help me or doing it to be hurtful. When I heard anything negative, I would shut down. There always seemed to be a specific pattern. For example, when I started a new job, I would always try to do everything right, without making any mistakes. The first time I did something stupid, and the supervisor would confront me, I would begin to have the same kinds of thoughts.

"You cannot do this job. You are not smart enough to figure everything out. You are not going to make it." Imagine if that is what went through your mind when you made any kind of mistake at all. I always had to hear positive things, or it would get me so messed up mentally that I would have a hard time keeping focused on what I was doing.

This was not only in secular things, but it was the same in the ministry. There were so many times that we would be out doing ministry, and something would be said about how things were not going very well. This would hit me like a ton of bricks. I remember having a feeling of numbness and losing any focus that I had. People would begin to come to me with all kinds of questions, and I know I appeared completely clueless. This was because I did not know how to handle criticism. A couple of things happened, which taught how important the right criticism was. I learned how to embrace it, and actually ask for it.

The first thing that happened, which helped me to embrace, and ask for, criticism, was something that I have already written about. It was when the coworkers, Marcus and Danny, I mentioned earlier had taken me under their wings, that I had begun to understand myself in a different light. I was able to make mistakes, and not completely lose all of my focus and confidence. I realized that having a different skill set did not make me stupid, it just meant that I brought something different to the table. It was through all the different abilities that we could work together and get positive results.

The second thing happened several months after I left that department, where I was working with Marcus and Danny. I had the opportunity to earn my Master of Business Leadership degree from Capella University. This degree drove home what I had been learning. All leaders were different, and this included their skill sets, and leadership styles.

At one point during this time, we really dug into the importance of constructive criticism. We were tasked with taking leadership review forms and having people who we were under us fill them out. The forms asked them to list the areas where I was strong, as well as the places where I needed work. At that time, I was a second shift supervisor, with 5 team leaders reporting to me.

By the time I had reached this point, I was becoming more aware that it was ok to accept the areas where I was weak. Also, I had slowly learned that just because someone said something negative about me, or my leadership, it did not mean that I had to completely shut down. Just because they may have been right about me being weak in some things, this did not mean that I was weak in every area.

To be honest, I think it was more difficult for some of those guys to fill out the forms, than it was for me to be willing to accept what they said about me. Even though I gave them the green light to be brutally honest, there were some who had trouble sharing what they felt was weak about me. It was not that they did not know of weaknesses, they just did not want to make me feel bad. Giving criticism is hard for some people to do.

I learned a great deal about myself from their responses. Although some were hesitant, they were willing to list things they felt I could work on. This did not bother me because I was more blown away by their positive responses. It made me realize that they cared for me as a leader, and their desire was for me to succeed.

After being in leadership for so many years, I had become aware of the areas where I did well. I also knew where I needed to get better. The thing that surprised me was just how many things they listed about my strengths, which I had not really thought much about. It did not fill me with pride, but it made me understand that God had equipped me to lead a certain way, and He was the one who gave me the strengths I needed, in order to succeed.

Our enemy really tries to get us to always think about the negative things people say about us. When we do that, it brings about discouragement, and makes it hard for us to be effective in ministry. My mother told me a story several years ago. It was about an evangelist, who had just given all he had in a service one night. After he finished preaching, he said that people gave him a standing ovation. He noticed one man, who had his arms folded with the most hateful look on his face. This man wanted the evangelist to know that he did not like what he preached. The rest of the night, the preacher was down, all because of that one person.

When pastors feel that they are being constantly criticized, getting down and out is pretty much guaranteed. If you have the right mindset, you can be that person who makes it clear to your pastor that you are there to help him through criticism, rather than bring him down by complaining. There are a couple of ways that you can do this.

First, you need to show your pastor that you care about his overall well-being. This is something that you can do on a regular basis, through your words and actions. Too many times, pastors only hear things from people when they have something to complain about. Let him know that you are praying for him. When you notice that he seems down, ask him if he is okay. Secondly, show your pastor that you want him to succeed in all that God has laid upon his heart. Rather than complaining about the organization, try to appreciate the vision that he has. Celebrate it with him. By doing this, he will realize that your criticism is constructive and meant to help him.

When I think of leaders who had the gift of giving criticism, the Apostle Paul always comes to mind. Just before he boldly, but lovingly, confronted the Corinthian church, in 1 Corinthians 1:4-9, he wrote these words,

> *I thank my God always concerning you for the grace of God which was given you in Christ Jesus, that in everything you were enriched in Him, in all speech and all knowledge, even as the testimony concerning Christ was confirmed in you, so that you are not lacking in any gift, awaiting eagerly the revelation of our Lord Jesus Christ, who will also confirm you to the end, blameless in the day of our Lord Jesus Christ. God is faithful, through whom you were called into fellowship with His Son, Jesus Christ our Lord.*

Wow! How in the world could you ever get mad at someone, when they express this kind of love for you? Paul's words let the church know that he cared about their well-being, and he wanted them to succeed. The Apostle even expressed his belief that they could be successful.

This passage reminds me of my late pastor, Bill, at Reed Springs. Every time I would do something crazy, or just plain stupid, he would see me, and yell, "Jamie, get over here!" I would go over and, in his deep, authoritative voice, with his 6 '4 height and wide shoulders, he would ask, "Son, what in the world were you thinking?" After all of that, he would put his arm around me, and with the biggest smile, he would say, "Son, you are doing a fine job. You are the best youth pastor around." I knew that Bill loved me, cared about my well-being, and wanted to see me succeed in all that I did. That is the kind of leader you accept critical criticism from.

Just like Bill, I realized early on, at Delano, that I had individuals who I could receive criticism from. The first person was the deacon I mentioned earlier, Steve. He is the Human Resource Director for a company with over 500 people. Day in and day out, he deals with people and problems. Because of this, he is excellent at being critical.

There were a couple of times, when I first became the pastor at Delano, that I was in meetings. One of those Steve was in, the other he was not. Both times, things were not going the way I thought they should, and people got very emotional, and so did I. Let's just say I did not react as a pastor should. It was not that I cussed anyone out, or took a swing at someone, but I seemed very angry. After those meetings, the same thing happened that always does after those situations, I felt horrible and defeated.

The days following those meetings, I called Steve, and asked him to coach me. He was very honest with me, but he did not jump on to me. Steve lovingly shared with me that he appreciated my passion. He said it was great having a pastor who was passionate about things. He then went on to give me ways to keep from getting in those positions and saying things I did not mean or would later regret.

A few months back, Steve and his wife met Mindy and I for dinner. At that time, we were going through some difficult things at church. I was very concerned about whether people were blaming me for some of the issues within the church. After I expressed my concerns to him, he looked me in the eye, and said something that I will never forget. "Jamie, it is my job to make sure that you succeed. If you fail, I fail. I am here to make sure that you succeed. We are in this together." At that moment, I realized something. There are thousands of pastors who would love to have that man as their deacon. It is because of moments like that, I have no trouble taking criticism from someone who loves me that much.

Steve is not the only guy who cares for me in that way. The entire group of deacons that God has blessed me with have been wonderful to me. We have had disagreements, but we have always been able to work it out. I gladly take criticism from those men because I know they have my best interest at heart.

I can say the same for the other leaders at Delano. One example is Dr. Cagle. When I became the pastor, he was actually the interim. He had entertained the idea of leaving once the church voted me in. I assured him that I did not have an issue with him staying, so he did, and I am so glad that he did. Every time I call on him, he is there to help me. He constantly encourages me, so criticism from him is always welcomed by me.

I also have other pastors, outside of Delano, who have been mentors to me, and they help guide me. The common denominator in all of these people is that I realize their desire is for me to succeed. They constantly encourage me and, when I need it, they throw in the criticism. By doing so, it doesn't feel like they are just coming down on me every time I make a mistake.

When thinking about the visionary pastor God has blessed you with, keep something in mind. He may or may not do good at receiving constructive criticism. If he doesn't, much of it may be because anytime anyone has ever criticized him, it felt more destructive, than constructive. Help your pastor by showing him that you are not out to hinder him or discourage him by always being negative. Remind him of the things that you appreciate and be gentle when you criticize.

Just like the people God has placed in my life, you may be the first person to show your pastor what genuine, constructive criticism is. It could be the key to bring about encouragement, as well as self-worth, so that he can lead your church to places that you never thought possible. Remember, feel free to criticize, but please make it constructive. Your pastor's overall well-being could depend on it.

Part Three
Specific Ways I have been Rescued

Chapter Eight

Having Prayer Partners I can be Vulnerable Around

Vulnerability can be difficult for everyone, especially senior pastors. Their job is to be the spiritual leader of an entire congregation. They are constantly in the spotlight, and the enemy really wants their weaknesses to be magnified. Because of that, many pastors have difficulty letting themselves become vulnerable around anyone.

However, for me, having literal teams of individuals so concerned about my success at Delano, that I can be completely vulnerable, is one of the reasons why I am learning to become the pastor God has called me to be. These are people that I can be real with and share pretty much every struggle I have. They don't judge me or have negative criticism. They surround me in prayer, and I feel it each day.

One of my favorite stories about prayer is in Acts 12:1-17. Simon Peter was in jail for doing God's work. The Bible tells us that the church began to pray for him. Peter didn't try to hide the fact that he was in jail, in a bad situation. They prayed without ceasing, and God sent an angel to get him out.

Don't you just love how when Peter got out of jail, he went to the place where they were praying, and beat on the door. The little gal who went to the door was so surprised to see him that she ran to tell everyone. Basically, they said, "You are crazy, leave us alone, we are praying that Peter gets out of jail."

While I have never been in jail, much less been in there for doing God's work, I have been in some very difficult places. Because I have been willing to be vulnerable with these teams of prayer warriors, they were able to cry out to God with specific requests for me. God is using them to help me move toward the goal of being the best visionary pastor that I could possibly be.

The first group is simply referred to as "The Prayer Group." While it is a basic name, there is nothing basic about it. If I were literally in a situation where I was on the verge of death, with no way out, I would call Sallie and get this group praying. And, regardless of what was going on in their lives at the time, they would stop and pray.

It all began very shortly after I had become the pastor at Delano. One Sunday morning, after I had finished preaching, one of the teenagers said someone wanted to meet me. She pointed toward this lady, who was in her 70's, with white hair, and a smile that lit up the room. She walked me back to her and said, "This is Sallie."

It was as if I had known Sallie for years, when we met that day. After meeting her, she went on to tell me about her prayer group. It was at her house, and they met every Tuesday at 10:00 a.m. The group is made up of ladies, mostly in their 70's and 80's, with one other man named Frankie. Frankie is a perfect example of the hands and feet of Christ.

After she told me all about the group, she asked me if I would be willing to come. I told her, "Of course!" She asked me when I could make it, and I said, "This coming Tuesday." I went that Tuesday, and I have never looked back. Every Tuesday morning (with a few exceptions), I have had the opportunity to go to this amazing prayer group.

As I was walking up Sallie's driveway that first Tuesday, I was excited, although I didn't really know what to expect. She had told me not to knock on the door, but to just walk on in. There would be coffee and sweets each week. When I walked in, everyone was seated, with big smiles on their faces. Sallie introduced me as the new pastor of Delano, who they had been praying for, for a long time.

There was a special seat in her living room. A lady named Margie used to sit in that seat. It had been a few years since Margie had been able to come to the prayer group. She was in assisted living, battling Dementia. They told me all about how special she was, and I was told that I could have that seat. Because Margie was a member of Delano, I had the opportunity to go spend some time with her at the place where she was staying. Even though she asked me who I was numerous times during my visits, I could still tell that she was, indeed, a special lady. I realized why even the chair I sat in had meaning.

When I sat down in that chair, I felt right at home. This was a prayer group which was made up of people from different churches, and denominations. A few of the ladies are members of Delano, so I at least knew some of them. I was told that there would be no discussion about politics, or gossip. Sallie is a stickler for those rules. Sometimes the conversation may appear to be heading in one of those directions, and we always get reeled back in.

That morning, Sallie began telling me about how they had prayed for me. She said, "We got word that Delano was looking for a pastor, so we started praying that God would send the right man. After a while, the name Jamie Johnson came up, as someone the pulpit committee was seriously considering. We started praying for you. After all that, here you are!" It is one thing to know that your friends pray for you, but it is even more awesome when people you had never met were sending up prayers on your behalf.

This group started treating me so special, much more special than I deserve. Besides praying, we always have a devotion, so she started getting me to do some of those. Sallie actually gave me the title, "Chaplain," which we all have fun joking about. They have taken me in as one of their own, and they really do understand the challenges that I, as a pastor, face.

With all of the things that happen on Tuesdays, the greatest is praying. One particular day, we were right in the middle of the devotion, and Sallie's phone rang. It was one of her friends from Michigan. Days before, Sallie's friend had sent an urgent prayer request, asking the prayer group to pray for. During the phone call, she told Sallie to let everyone know how grateful she was. God had just answered the prayers.

During these times, we will often have a special guest. These are people that Sallie, and her late husband, Bill, have known for years. These were always individuals that they had been ministry partners with. One Tuesday, a man named Richard was at the prayer group. He did an amazing job sharing the devotion. When he finished, Sallie told us that he and his wife were trying to sell their house, and it had been on the market for a long time. We prayed about it that day.

Sallie called me early the next week and said that not only had his house sold, but it was a God thing, concerning how it all happened. She told me that Richard would be coming back to share the story. I think it was a couple of weeks later that he came.

Once the prayer group started, he told us the story. After so many months, Richard had gotten an offer on his house. It was not exactly what they wanted, but they were going to take it. After they sat down with their agent, just before they signed, Richard got a phone call. It was someone else, who made a much better offer. Talk about happening just on time! This was not the first time that they prayed for a house to sell, and it did. In fact, because of their prayers, my own house sold, and we were able to see an impossible deal come through for us to get the house we currently live in.

Although these things have been amazing for me to witness, and be a part of, the fact that I have been able to be so vulnerable has been the greatest thing for me. One Sunday after church, my family was having lunch. My son was living on his own at the time, so he met us at the restaurant. I do not remember why, but I was in an extremely bad mood when we got there. Austin and I got into a conversation, in which we disagreed about some things. I lost my cool, and I said some very hurtful things to him. Of course I was loud, so everyone around me could hear what I said.

We left that place, and things were very bad. I had not only hurt him, but I crushed my wife. I don't know what my daughter was feeling at that moment, but it could not have been good. It was not long after we left that I got that sick feeling in my stomach. Very few times have I seen my wife hurting like that. Finally, she was able to forgive me, and so was my son.

That next Tuesday, I went to the prayer group. I told them everything that had happened, and how I did not feel fit to be a pastor. How could I preach to my congregation and, an hour later, treat my son like I did, as well as hurt my wife and daughter? Those ladies, and Frankie, did not tell me how horrible I was. They were honest about how I should not have done what I did, but they loved on me.

I opened up to them about how there have been other times that I got agitated and done similar things. I let them know that I wanted to get past that and quit allowing my emotions to get the best of me. Sallie had me go to the center of the living room, and I felt hands all over my back. They prayed for me that God would help me to overcome these things. From that moment on, I began to notice how God was helping me be more in control in those situations. While I have gotten better at not letting my passion and emotions control my actions, I am not exactly where I want to be yet. However, because God has used the prayers of this group, I am not where I was either.

One Tuesday morning, roughly a year after I had been going to the prayer group, I walked in the house, and there was a new lady there. Her name is Lynn. Sallie told us about meeting her at the grocery store and inviting her to come. When Lynn first started talking, I knew there was something special about her. She is extremely wise, and has a great understanding of Scripture, and man can she pray! Besides me, Sallie has recruited her to help share devotions. Lynn is also from a Pentecostal background and has served in churches in associate pastoral roles. Her teaching of Scripture is better than some male pastors I have heard.

Not long into her being a part of the group, Lynn began to greatly encourage me, as a pastor. One Tuesday she brought in a small journal, which recorded the prayers that she had prayed for me. She would often tell me that God had me at Delano church to make a huge difference, as well as to be an impact for the entire community. Eventually, she started attending our church, and has been an encouragement to all of us. Often, she will send me texts showing how God spoke to her about encouraging me. It is always from God's Word, and always what I need at the time.

Lynn has testified at the prayer group and told us that God had really done work in her heart. He had revealed to her that Christians need to focus on the things that bring us together, rather than those that divide us. She said that even the idea of her going to a Baptist church came about as a result of God getting her beyond her comfort zones. I am so glad that He has, and that she is so obedient. One situation shows the power of her prayer life.

One Friday, I called Pat, and asked him if he wanted to go with me to visit some older church members. All day we heard great things. People just went on and on about how good things were happening at Delano. It was one encouraging situation after another. That is, until we went to the last house.

For the first few minutes, everything was going well. All of our discussions were good. Then, I told the couple that we were visiting that we had to go, so we prayed. After the prayer, the husband and wife began to complain about our church. They talked about several of the members, and they were extremely critical (and not constructive). I held my cool, but I let them know that I totally disagreed with them, and I think they realized I didn't appreciate what they were saying. Pat and I went to the car as fast as we could.

Just before we got in the car, I said to him, "If you ever want to know what will bring a pastor down, and discourage him, that was it." Even though we had been showered with compliments and encouragement for hours prior to that, all of the complaining and negativity took a toll on me that day, and all weekend. It was difficult to get the stuff out of my head, so I prayed as much as I could about it and told the Lord that I just had to depend on Him. He got me through, and over, it by Sunday.

On Monday, I talked to Sallie. What she told me blew my mind. On Friday morning, the same day Pat and I visited, Lynn called Sallie and told her to put on a pot of coffee. Neither ladies knew what I was doing that day, much less what had happened. When she got there, Lynn told Sallie that I was being spiritually attacked, and they needed to pray for me. So, while Pat and I were dealing with all of the complaining about our church (which is some of the most difficult spiritual attacks pastors face) I had two ladies getting in touch with God on my behalf, and they had no idea what was going on. As a pastor, those kinds of things are more valuable than any amount of money someone might give you.

After many Tuesdays, the prayer group saw just how much of a visionary that I was. I would go in and talk to them about my plans for the church, and what all I wanted to get done. I remember Sallie saying many times, "Jamie, you better slow down." They always joke about being, "White-haired mamas to me." That is exactly what they are. There have been so many times that I walked in on Tuesday, discouraged. I was discouraged because I tried to get too many things going, simply because I could visualize, but I lacked the organization. Each time, they would do what they always do. They would lift me up in prayer, and I mean, they prayed! Every time I would edge closer to not making the same old mistakes.

I have said this many times, "I have been in the ministry for over 20 years, but I did not understand the power of prayer in the same way I have since I have been a part of the prayer group." Visionary pastors need people like this. Those they can be vulnerable with, and trust with all of their shortcomings. They need individuals who can get in touch with God like no one else. He will use their prayers to help lead them in the way He has called them, as well as help them find the right people to come alongside them, so that their visions will succeed. I am seeing this happen before my very own eyes.

Besides the prayer group, there is another team of men, who I believe pray for me, daily. That group is my deacons. I have worked with deacons for many years, but my experience with them at Delano has been one of a kind.

When I first became the pastor, I didn't really have the kind of understanding of the deacon's role, as I should. So many times, in the Baptist church, the group of deacons have been viewed more like a Board of Directors. However, concerning the office of the position, in NAS New Testament Greek Lexicon, the word deacon is defined in one of the following ways, "a deacon, one who, by virtue of the office assigned to him by the church, cares for the poor and has charge of and distributes the money collected for their use."[7]

A passage often used to preach deacon's ordination services is found in Acts 6:1-4,

> *Now at this time while the disciples were increasing in number, a complaint arose on the part of the Hellenistic Jews against the native Hebrews, because their widows were being overlooked in the daily serving of food. So the twelve summoned the congregation of the disciples and said, "It is not desirable for us to neglect the word of God in order to serve Tables. Therefore, brethren, select from among you seven men of good reputation, full of the Spirit and of wisdom, whom we may put in charge of this task. But we will devote ourselves to prayer and to the ministry of the word* (NASB).

In this passage, when dealing with the men who were chosen, the question is, "Were these men considered deacons?" The *Bible Believer's Commentary* answers this question well, by saying, "Although these men are not designated deacons in the Bible, it is not unreasonable to think of them as such. In the expression, **serve tables**, the word **serve** is the verb form of the noun from which we get the English word *deacon*, so their function literally was to

---

7 Diakonos, Bible Study Tools, https://www.biblestudytools.com/lexicons/greek/nas/diakonos.html, accessed February 18, 2022.

"deacon" tables." [8] Regardless of what one thinks about a deacon's role, one thing is clear, they are to be servants to the body of Christ.

When I first became the pastor, I had spent a great deal of time with one of my mentors which I mentioned earlier, retired pastor Dr. Dennis Cagle. Before I came to Delano, when he was the interim, Dennis had been working with Steve, concerning the need for deacons to be more like servants than CEO's, and the need to develop a deacon family plan.

Knowing this, I went into the church with the wrong mindset. I wanted these guys to understand their roles as servants so much that I forgot about equipping them to be leaders. There were times when I should have allowed them to lead in certain areas, and I actually worked against them. There definitely is a fine line between being a servant and being a leader. In the role of deacons, both things must happen.

A few months into my pastorate, Dennis offered to conduct deacon training. We were able to get everyone on board and, in one long weekend, he conducted it. It would be through that training that I realized what I had done wrong. Because these guys were servants to the church, it was their job to make decisions that had to do with the unity and overall wellbeing of the body of Christ. I learned that these guys needed to be my support staff, which I could go to with anything. Before I make any major decision, I go to those guys first. Together, we make decisions that we feel are best for the entire body.

Besides learning these things, I also realized that I need these guys to be my prayer partners. Once the training was over with, I went to them. I apologized for how I had led before, and I let them know how much I needed them. We took a major leap forward, and our relationship is growing stronger the more I work with these guys. They understand my flaws, and my issues with organization, and they are in my corner, praying for me, and helping me become a better leader.

Just like I have been able to be vulnerable with the prayer group, I can do the same with these men. When I am feeling discouraged, I tell them. When I am concerned about things going on in my family, I don't hide what it is. I tell them, so they can pray with specificity,

---

8 MacDonald, *Believer's Bible Commentary*, 1601.

and they do. Before COVID19, they were meeting me in the front of the sanctuary before church began, and they prayed over me. I don't feel that there is anything about my ministry that I have to hide from these guys. The best thing of all, I have a group of men who have been able to forgive me for not being the leader I should have been, and they are praying for me, and helping me become the pastor God has called me to be.

Another group, which I will briefly mention, is other pastors. Just like the prayer group, there are men from other denominations (though similar in beliefs), who meet on a regular basis. We come together with one thing on our minds. How can we help each other promote the Gospel throughout our communities?

Besides different denominations, we have different ethnic backgrounds as well. In a year where we have watched a great deal of division within our country, it is awesome to be able to come together in unity with these guys. As a result, we have had the opportunity to do various projects together.

In some of our planning meetings, we have ended up having unplanned prayer meetings. After a few weeks of getting together with these guys, I realized something. Regardless of what age each one was, or how long they had been in the ministry, everyone was fighting the same battles, with many of the same struggles.

What I appreciate about these guys is that no matter what we have come together to do, when they sense someone is struggling, the meeting becomes all about calling on heaven, on behalf of that individual. Just like with these other groups, I have been completely honest with them about my struggles. At the last couple of meetings, I shared the problems I have had due to me being such a strong visionary. Once I did, I found out that most of the guys struggled with the same things. Now I know that I have a group of pastors who are praying for me, so that I can surround myself with people who will contribute to my success.

Finally, there is no way that I could ever mention prayer partners, which I can be vulnerable with, without talking about Mindy. There is nothing my wife does not know about me. She has watched me struggle many times. Through all of that, she is still my biggest fan. The other day she told me, "Jamie, it just hit me. I have not spent enough time praying for you. I pray for you, but I haven't prayed hard enough for you lately. I spend a lot of time praying for our children, but I am going to spend a lot more time praying for you." That was enough to get my spiritual engine running on all cylinders.

Visionary pastors need prayer partners. Not just people saying that they will pray for them, but people who take the time to listen to them. These prayer partners must be trustworthy, and willing to allow their pastors to be vulnerable about their struggles. I can honestly say, when I walk in Sallie's house, or meet in a room with those deacons and pastors, I am free to be who I am. There is no concern about someone walking out the door and gossiping about me, and what I am dealing with. Because of this, those groups are trustworthy, and they allow me to be vulnerable. Both of which are highly important.

If your pastor does not have a group like this, please form one. As you look for others to join you, make sure they are trustworthy, caring, and know how to get in touch with God. Find a time when you and the group can meet with the pastor and begin praying intentionally for him and his success. By doing so, God will do amazing things through your group, and pastor, which will be impossible to explain by human means!

Chapter Nine

Becoming More Fond of Delegation

I have been given the amazing privilege of going to Israel a couple of times. The second time was January of 2020, and it was the most memorable for me, for a number of reasons. For one thing, my wife had the opportunity to go, which did not happen on my first trip. I cannot begin to describe the joy I had when standing beside Mindy in places such as Mount Carmel. You will remember that this location was where Elijah challenged the false prophets, and God brought down fire from the sky (1 Kings 18). Standing in that amazing place with my wife was one of many things that happened on that trip.

One of the greatest takeaways were the two times that God spoke very clearly to me. The first was in the Garden of Gethsemane, and the second was on the southern steps of the Temple. Our Director of Missions, Tony, led the trip. It was him who made sure that we took some time to seek God in both of those locations. I am so thankful that he did.

The Garden of Gethsemane is a gorgeous place, filled with olive trees and awesome scenery. Just beyond, and not very far away, is the remains of Herod's Temple. It is amazing to see that everything within the story of Jesus' death, burial, and resurrection, is so close. That is something that has surprised everyone I have talked to about their first trip, including me.

When we walked into the Garden, Tony instructed us to find a location, and to get alone with God. As I was finding the perfect place, I watched as people on our trip were worshiping. Some were very still with little outward emotion. Others had tears flowing down their cheeks. Regardless of how we all responded, one thing was clear, God's presence was evident.

As I began to pray, I felt as though I was being impressed to seek God concerning my leadership as the pastor of Delano. It was as if the Lord was reminding me that my focus needed to be much more limited than what it had been. Instead of just leading people, I had gotten back in the habit of feeling like my hands had to be in everything. It was as if God was saying what my wife always reminded me, "Your job is to preach, and love on your people. You need to let other people do their job as well."

I remember really pouring out my heart to God, letting Him know that I was clear on what He wanted me to do, but I just did not know if I had it in me. Don't you just love that word, but, followed by our excuses? I cannot even believe that we have the audacity to say "but" to God, instead of "Yes, oh Lord!" As soon as I finished praying, I walked over to a spot where I could just look at the Temple. In front of me was the Eastern Gate. Immediately, a thought crossed my mind, and I knew it was the Lord. "You are standing in a place of agony, and you are gazing on the place of guaranteed victory."

Without a doubt, I was in a place that could be described as agony. Prior to being arrested, Jesus went into this place to pray. We all know that His prayers were so intense, that "His sweat became like great drops of blood" (ESV). Also, it was the place where He cried out to the Father, that the Father's will be done. Our Lord Jesus would then begin the process where He would be tried, whipped, mocked, and eventually be crucified for our sins. It would be because of this that you and I have been able to receive the free gift of grace. It is understandable why the only description that came to me that day was, it was a place of agony.

This gate, however, was different. According to my understanding of Eschatology, I believe that King Jesus will walk through the Eastern Gate when He returns the second time (Ezekiel 44:1-3). It will be at that time that He will sit on the Throne and be crowned King of Kings and Lord of Lords. As I stood there looking at this amazing site, I began to think about all the things that mankind has destroyed. I sensed God reminding me that although people can mess up a lot of things, when it comes to God's promises, we cannot hinder any of them from coming to pass.

It was at this point that God said to me, "Jamie, after I left this place of agonizing prayer, I was able to do everything that had to be done, in order to save you through the power of the Gospel. Also, my promise to return is guaranteed to be fulfilled, regardless of what happens in the world. Is that not enough to convince you that I can help you be what I have called you to be, and do what I am asking you to do?"

For me, this resonated in a certain way. Mankind has a way of messing everything up, and I mean everything. That day, I realized, if it were possible, we would definitely find a way to keep God's salvation of our souls from happening. Leave it up to us and we would find a way to stop the return of Jesus. But, because this is God's promise, it will not fail. Just as much as He has the power to fulfill that great promise, He has the power to help me lead Delano church in the way He has called me. You can't argue with God when you are standing in a place of agony, gazing on a place of victory.

The second time that I sensed God speak was a few days after that. We went to the famous southern steps of the Temple. After sharing some very insightful information, Tony asked us to find a place on the steps to spend time talking to the Lord, asking Him what He wanted to show us. God definitely showed me something.

I walked over to a particular place, and I bowed. I closed my eyes, and I asked God to help me clear my head, and I asked Him to speak to me. God brought a Biblical person to mind, which I mentioned very early in the book, Nehemiah. When Nehemiah led the team back to Jerusalem, in order to rebuild the walls (the book of Nehemiah) a lot of people had different jobs to do. I sensed God reminding me of that. He said, "In that story, there were builders and other workers. Everyone did what they were supposed to do, and the job was accomplished."

Besides rebuilding the walls, during the return, the Temple was rebuilt, the Law was instituted, and revival took place. I opened my eyes there on those steps, and it hit me, "I am in the place where God sent Judah home, and I am on the steps of the Temple!" The very city we were in, was where the story of Ezra and Nehemiah happened. God reminded me of what I had prayed about in Gethsemane.

I needed to focus on what He had called me to do and allow everyone else in the church to do their part. Even if they did it differently than I would have, I needed to get out of their way. I became very excited that day. I knew God had spoken to me clearly, and now it was time for me to listen. The question after leaving that hit me was, "How in the world was I going to get that done?" The answer, learn to be a better delegator.

As I mentioned earlier, Nehemiah was a visionary, but he did not try to make things happen on his own. He had an entire team of individuals that jumped in and got the job done. In chapter 2:11-18 we see that Nehemiah surveys the walls, and he really got a good understanding of the situation. In chapter 3, people got to work. Everyone had a clear understanding of what their job was, and they did what they were supposed to. Even though they faced conflict, the walls were eventually built (Nehemiah 6:15).

If your visionary pastor is going to succeed, without losing his mind, delegation is a must. Whenever pastors have clear visions from God, just like Nehemiah did, making sure that this vision comes to pass is way too much for one person. This process is not the easiest thing to do, but it is necessary. With God's help, there are ways that your visionary pastor can learn to be a delegator.

The first thing that you can encourage him to do, and the most important, is to pray. For people like me, delegation does not come easy. I am always afraid that people will feel like I am putting too many demands on them. Also, it is not easy to know who to ask. Other times, it just seems easier to just do it myself. I am learning that it never really is. Reminding your pastor of the importance of praying for the right people that he can delegate things to, are important. You can also let him know that you are joining him in prayer as well.

I am continually learning the importance of praying for the right people to help me. That is what we have been commanded to do. In Matthew 9:36-38, the Bible says, "Seeing the people, He felt compassion for them, because they were distressed and dispirited like sheep without a shepherd. Then He said to His disciples, "The harvest is plentiful, but the workers are few. Therefore beseech the Lord of the harvest to send out workers into His harvest" (NASB).

Jesus does not tell Christians to get up on Sunday morning, during announcements, and beg people to come help out in certain ministries. He tells us to pray that God would send us laborers. I am not saying that we stop asking people. However, I am saying that we should do what is most effective. We need to pray. Through that prayer, God will begin to open the doors so that the right people will either volunteer, or God will lead you to approach them. I have witnessed this lately.

Besides reinforcing the importance of praying for laborers, helping him find people to ask would be a great benefit to him as well. Lately, I am finding out more and more that there are people in my church, who are willing to do just about anything. That is, if I ask. For many years, I would just ask for volunteers, and that may have worked early on. It just does not seem to work in today's times. Now people are more inclined to help when you ask them.

It seems that there is so much to do, and nowhere near enough volunteers to get it all done. Pastors everywhere are begging people to help them. The visionary pastor is no different. Many times God will lay the vision on his heart, and he works to finally get buy-in. However, once he starts to put everything in motion, he realizes that things are not going as we hoped because of a lack of help.

Your pastor needs to think like Nehemiah, when he sees the big job ahead of him. He didn't try to do it on his own, at any time. Nehemiah 3 shows that he had all kinds of talented people around him. Your pastor has people in your church who can help him. Encourage him to begin doing what Jesus told Christians to do, pray for workers. After that, let him know that asking people to help is necessary. Also, be the kind of person who helps him enlist talented workers.

In Nehemiah 8, Ezra had the opportunity to stand and read the Law. If he had been pulled away, in order to do manual labor, or take care of other things, we may not have the amazing story of revival which followed his reading of God's Word. Let your pastor visualize, and lead, but make sure he understands the power of delegating.

Chapter Ten

Having the Right Team is Essential

Even though my favorite sport to watch now is college football, which was not true as a kid. In fact, I could not have cared less about football then. I loved the NBA. I remember begging my mother to let me stay up late when the finals were on. Those battles between Magic Johnson's Lakers and Larry Bird and the Celtics were what I always looked forward to. I was a diehard Celtics fan. Unfortunately, by the time I got into it, the Celtics were at the end of their run. The Lakers were king.

A few years later, this young player came on the scene. I am sure you have heard of him, Michael Jordan. I know there has been much debate over whether he was the best basketball player of all time. Most people around my age seem to agree. There are some who would disagree. The young people who feel it is Lebron, you have the right to have a wrong opinion, which is my opinion.

A few months back, ESPN did a special called "The Last Dance." Mindy and I watched every episode. If you saw that, it would be hard to argue that Jordan was not the best of all time. He told people what he was going to do to other players and teams the next day, and he always did it!!! It was as if he could predict what he would do to you and, no matter what you did, you could not stop him.

Even though he was very good, arguably the greatest, one thing was certain, he could not win championships without teammates. It took guys like Pippen helping score points, Rodman getting rebounds, and Paxon as the floor general. Jordan may get most of the glory, but 6 rings came because they played as a team. Just like with athletes, if visionary pastors are going to succeed, they must have people on their team. As I shared in the previous chapter, your visionary pastor needs to be a great delegator. Choosing the right team is one part of that process.

Sports fans know what a successful sports team looks like. But, what does it look like when pastors have the right people on their team? At Delano we have wonderful deacons and committees making sure that things get done. But, for the purpose of this chapter, I want to zone in on a certain team. I have other pastor friends who call this team the "dream team." Another pastor friend of mine calls his team "the task force." The reason for that name; he wants to make sure that people understand that the team is about actually getting things done.

For visionary pastors like me, I need to have a specific team of people, who will listen to the visions that God has placed on my heart. I need to be able to throw everything at them, and have these people help me organize, and put feet on what God is leading our church, through me, to do. Often I have been told that I share my visions with the entire church much faster than I should. Having the right team has helped me stop doing that.

I tell all the members of this team that I need them to listen to me and understand that I will share a whole lot of stuff. In fact, in every meeting, we are always figuring out how much unnecessary stuff is in there and, believe me, there always is. The great thing about this team is that they are more than willing to listen to everything I tell them, because I am willing to take their constructive criticism.

For me, my visions are always focused on outreach and discipleship. In every church where I have served, my passion has always been to lead people into missions. I let all the other things be taken care of without getting overly concerned with it. But missions! I have always considered that my baby.

The problem with me just planning all of it is that we end up in the same situations as I always have. We have more things to do than the people to do it. By meeting with the team behind closed doors, we can discuss all the resources needed to make missions happen before it even gets out to the rest of the church.

Of course, when I first became the pastor, I had no idea that I needed a team to help me with this. Because the church was full of workers, and I was full-time, I just thought that we could take off. After ending up in the same position that I had always ended up in, I realized that something must change. At a small group meeting one night, the idea of a dream team came up.

It was at this point that I began talking to the people that I felt comfortable being on this team. We came together, and things felt right. There was still a little problem, and my wife saw it clearly. Even though I was sold on letting the team take a lot of responsibility away from me, I didn't know how to get out of everyone's way! Allow me to illustrate how my wife makes fun of me.

My wife always makes fun of me because I love dry erase boards! One particular time, I had an idea about some local outreach. I told Pat that I would like to share with the team at his house during the next small group. Unlike me, Pat always tries to be behind the scenes. He loves it when I am running the show. Apparently (according to my sweet Mindy) so do I! In reality, I think I just feel like I know how everything should always go.

That Thursday night at Pat's house, I made sure that I had a dry erase board. I had everyone gather round, and I was writing all the things on there that I wanted us to do. No one really had much to say, other than the fact that they liked what I was talking about. I walked away with my chest stuck out as the dude who had it all figured out. That is, until we got in the car.

Once again, Mindy saw the problem. "Jamie, why are you always the one trying to control everything? You need to let other people take charge." I really didn't like what she had to say. Since then, I have learned that she is exactly right. Even though I put a lot of energy into that presentation, it was just another dream, among many, which did not ever come to fruition.

For visionary pastors like myself, it is just so difficult to let go. Not only do we have the vision, but we feel like we know how it should be brought about. However, God has shown me some things lately on what it means to really let go. I used to think that it meant to loosen my grip. I was wrong. Letting go means to completely turn loose.

A few months ago, we were on vacation in Charleston, S.C. I had really been working on trying to surrender everything to God, and allow my people to take things on, without me interfering. One day, I was in the Atlantic Ocean. I was talking to God. God showed me that taking my hands off meant both hands. It meant to completely surrender. It's hard to argue with God when you are standing in something that can only be explained by, "God created this ocean."

Sometime after our vacation, something happened that made me feel like I might be moving in the right direction. I pulled together a group of like-minded people and met at the church. This is a group of people who, like me, are dead set on seeing people saved and discipled. Before I knew it, we were sitting in a room with my dry-erase board. Have I told you that I love those things? I started by opening up the meeting, and everyone joined in.

It was not long before I realized that these folks had way better ideas than me. Typically in the past, I would have still been trying to force my ideas down everyone's throats. This time it hit me. I needed to get away from the board and shut up. That is exactly what happened. I even left the room for a little while to do something else. By the time I came back, this team already had the ideas together. I am excited about seeing the things God will do through our outreach/discipleship ministry. I realized that we had the "dream team" that was going to make these visions come to pass.

Visionary pastors need talented teams to help them accomplish the visions that God has placed on their hearts. For me, this has been a process, which I have not mastered. Even though I have not mastered it, I praise God that He has helped me get better at it. Having the team around your pastor, to ensure that his weaknesses do not stop the vision from coming to fruition is necessary. For me, I look for visionaries, as well as organizers. I also look for people who will say to me, "Pastor, I love the idea, but we may need to look at a better way of making it happen." I don't need yes men on my team.

You may be the person to suggest to your pastor that he needs this kind of a team. You may also be someone that he needs on his team. There are many pastors today, who feel like every vision they have will never be fulfilled. Some just need people to walk up to them and say, "pastor, I love your vision, and I am sold on it. Let's put together a group of individuals that you can trust, who will ensure that it happens." That may be all your pastor needs to help lead your church to be the force that God has called it to be.

Part Four
Learning to Let Him Do What I Cannot

Chapter Eleven
Learning to Trust the Process

After having watched tons of college football coaches being interviewed, I have heard a lot of those guys say the same stuff. For anyone who follows the sport, you know exactly what I am talking about. All of those guys have certain sayings that are common among them. One of those things I have heard over and over is, "I have told the players and fans that you have to trust the process."

This always happens when a coach is new to the program, and he wants to bring in a new system. I guess I have heard this so much because of all the times a new coach has made that comment, when being introduced as the head football guy at the University of Tennessee, since Philip Fulmer was fired in 2008. We have had way too many coaching changes.

The idea for trusting the process is that because everything is new, it will take some time for the team to be where the coaches and fans want them to be. There is so much that goes into the process to make it effective. Coaches must recruit the right players, get the players to buy into the particular system that they are running, and make it all work on Saturdays. As the visionary pastor at Delano, God has been showing me that I must trust His process.

Going back to that day I was in the Atlantic Ocean; I was seeking God for direction. It was then that the thought of trusting the process crossed my mind for the first time. Even though I heard Him loud and clear, this idea about trusting the process did not really resonate with me until after I returned and ended up in some of the same situations. I will dare say that I am still learning how to make that happen.

A few weeks after we returned from vacation, we ran into some situations where important decisions had to be made. I will not mention specifics. I was being confronted by a lot of different people. I did the same thing that I usually do, I wrestled with what I needed to do. I felt the pressure as if it were my job, and mine only, to fix this thing. I talked to Mindy about it, and her reply, "Let your committees handle everything." I knew she was right, but I still wrestled with it. Most of the time the struggles happened when I was trying to go to sleep. Pretty common among all of us.

I would lay in my bed and toss and turn, worried about what I should do. I remember each time, that small, still, voice (1 Kings 18), saying, "Trust the process." I was trying very hard. It would be soon after that, that God would begin doing a work in my heart, so that I would finally start applying this, and it happened through some powerful situations. You will see that some of those were not what anyone would have asked for, but it was what God used.

The first one was when I met with the committee who handled the things that we were facing. One of the women on that committee, Rhonda, has been telling me, "You are the spiritual leader in our church! It is not your job to handle all of these problems!" Everyone else on the committee agreed. At that meeting, we agreed that if there was an issue brought to me, I needed to redirect the person to the committee that handled it. After the meeting we prayed that I would do that, and that God would lead the committee.

The Lord revealed to me that one of the main ways to trust the process meant turning things over to people who had volunteered to handle them and turning it completely over to them. I say that because even in times past, when I thought I had turned things over, I would still hang on to them just a little bit. Rhonda was clear, let go. As God said, "Trust the process."

Shortly after that, we had a situation where a key member, and leader in our church left. For all of those individuals who are not pastors, which is really hard to take. In fact, any time someone from the church leaves, the pastor always questions if it was his fault. He will ask himself over and over, "Was there something different I could have done?" "At the end of the day, did I do something offensive to cause this person to leave?" No matter what anyone tells him, he will always question what he could have done differently.

This was not the first person who had left the church, but the position this person held was very important, and not easily filled. As soon as this happened, I remember thinking, "What if other people feel like I'm a major problem here?" "What if we have a mass exodus, and the church shrinks down to almost no one coming?" You may be thinking that those kinds of questions are a bit of a stretch, but I would guess that all pastors have had them.

As I would allow those thoughts to plague me, it would bring me to a point of discouragement, and I would often feel like I was in a hopeless situation. During the darkest of those times, I would hear, "Trust the process." I knew this was what I needed to do, but knowing what needed to be done, and doing it, were two very different things.

I remember a couple of times when all of this was going on, that I had a thought I had never had. It went like this, "You cannot do this any longer!" There had been many times in the ministry when I had wanted to give up, but this time it was different. This time I was starting to entertain the thought that I was incapable of being a good pastor. It was as if the entire church world was against me, and I did not have it in me to come out of this thing successfully.

God is so good, and He speaks to us in the darkest of times. The thing that kept me going was His voice. It wasn't audible, by no means. I remember hearing Charles Stanley say this, "Does God speak audibly to you?" His answer, "no, He speaks louder than that." In those discouraging times, at the very moment when I didn't think I could continue, I heard God scream to my spirit, "Trust the process!" It was then that something clicked. The reason God was telling me to trust the process was because there would be times when it did not seem to be working. God was reminding me that while it did not look good at the time, He was still in control and working.

The next situation I'll mention was nothing short of amazing. It happened at the time when trusting the process was starting to really click. A few months back, my chairman of deacons, Chuck, texted me. He wanted to meet with me and discuss something that God had placed on his heart. We agreed to meet at Hardee's the following Tuesday. The Sunday before, I was driving to church, and a thought hit me. It was all about revival, but not in the sense that I had always known.

From the time I can remember, revival meant one thing. For 2 or 3 days, up to a week, church services were scheduled. There was singing and preaching. The goal was that by the end of the week, we all experienced revival. Even though I had been a part of great revival meetings, some I had the opportunity to preach in, this was not the kind of thing God was laying on my heart. This time, I was just thinking about experiencing a life-changing event, instead of a series of meetings.

That Tuesday came, and Chuck and I met. Not long after we sat down, he said God had been speaking to him about revival. He went on to say, "Not revival in the normal sense." You can imagine how what he said affected me. At that moment, I knew God was up to something.

Within a couple of hours, we had a meeting laid out. Basically, the whole service was going to be focused on worship and prayer. Chuck works swing shifts, and a lot of those days are on Sundays. The date that we were both thinking, he was going to be off. Talk about God's timing. We had it set up to have certain people sing, and others come forward and pray about specific things the enemy had been attacking us all with. We even titled it "One day prayer and revival service."

That Sunday I woke up at 5am, and I was wide awake. I felt a sense of excitement and anticipation. I went into the living room and began to pray. Throughout my prayer time, I could tell that God was going to do big stuff, and big stuff He did!

The service started with Chuck coming forward and sharing how God had placed this one-day revival on his heart. After that, I shared with the church how God had been challenging me to "Trust the process." I told them that I had tried to do more than God called me to do, and that I needed to get out of His way, by letting other people take responsibility. I made a commitment that Sunday that my leadership would look much different from that day forward.

There is just something about a pastor confessing something before the whole church. It creates a strong sense of accountability. Now, every time I think about doing things the old way, I am reminded of what I shared with the church that day. It definitely helps me stay on track.

The service was more amazing than I had even thought it would be. After I shared my heart, I had the deacons come forward and I prayed over each of them by name. Afterward, they prayed over me. My mentor, Dennis, came forward to pray over me. He even got Mindy up there, and he prayed the most amazing prayer over us.

One of the women in our church, who can sing like a bird, sang the song, "What a wonderful name it is." It was at that point that the service really broke loose. People started coming to the altar to pray. Other people were giving powerful testimonies about how God had restored their marriages, and some talked about breaking free from depression. It was one of the most awesome services that I have ever been a part of. In the days following, it was starting to resonate with me that this process was something that was worth trusting. It may not have always felt that way, but that service showed me that God was working even when it didn't feel like it.

When having the kind of revival service that we had, it is easy to start thinking that smooth sailing is ahead. In the following days after the revival, I heard so many great things. People were just going on and on about how great that service was and how God had moved. Just to put things in perspective, the service was over 2 hours long, and no one was ready to leave. For Baptist folks, which is big! It was an encouraging time in my ministry. I hate to admit this, but I almost felt as though the enemy was whipped so badly that Delano was not going to have any more major issues. Deep down I knew that was not the case, but that is how it felt.

A few months after that wonderful Sunday, we had another situation that was discouraging to me. Just like the earlier one I mentioned, it had to do with a small group of people leaving the church. The problem with these situations is the enemy wants to bring you back to thinking about all of the other people that had left. When the enemy would bring those things back up to me, God would always remind me, "trust the process."

I am not going to say that I will ever reach a place where I will master trusting God completely, by trusting the process. However, through these situations, and the ones I will mention in the last chapter, I feel I am learning the importance of this more than I ever have. God is doing amazing things that are showing me that the process can be trusted. I will conclude the book by sharing a couple of those. While these things are not always easy, when God is doing the work, the result is always wonderful.

Trust the process is something that most all of us have heard before. You may be like me and have heard it from coaches, or you may have heard it from other places. For some time now, this is something that God has been reminding me to do as a pastor. It seems like the times when I felt like I couldn't go any further, this thought was the strongest.

Little did I know, during those tough times, that His process was one that was going to make me a better visionary pastor. His plan was to bring the people I needed into Delano (which would replace some of those who had left) so that I could focus on the things that He has called me to do. In the final chapter, I will show you the amazing things that God has done, and is still doing, in fulfilling His plan at Delano. This chapter was all about learning to trust His process. The final chapter is about trusting His provision.

Every visionary pastor, and those serving with him need to understand something. God has a plan for every church. He wants these pastors to do what He has called them to do, and let others do their part. Learning to do everything the Lord's way, and not ours, is not always easy.

If your pastor has trouble allowing people to do their jobs, you may need to come alongside him and guide him. If your pastor is like me, he feels as though he knows what needs to be done, and how to do it. Giving up that control is not always easy, but it is necessary. I am thankful for the people at Delano who understand my struggles, and they have been willing to be honest with me as well as take some of these responsibilities off of me. This is part of trusting God's process.

Another aspect of trusting God's plan for your specific church is realizing that some people, in important positions, are going to leave. Often it is because they have different philosophies than the pastor, or they just cannot support the vision that God has given him. Sometimes people just leave for weird reasons. You may need to encourage him to stay the course. Let him know that just because people leave, it doesn't handcuff God and keep Him from moving.

Help your pastor understand that if God has given him a vision for the church, God will bring it about, as long as he stays close to Him. Don't let him get discouraged by what others do or don't do, or even who is or is not at church on Sunday. As I was driving to Delano one Sunday morning, God spoke to me. He said this, "You worry about preaching to your people, and I will worry about who shows up, and who doesn't." Remember, God doesn't need any of us to fulfill any mission or vision that He gives us for the church. Tell your pastor to never stop trusting the process.

Chapter Twelve

Learning to Trust in God's Provision

Growing up in the amazing decades of the 80's and 90's, we were taught not to throw away food. Every time I started to throw anything away, I would hear, "There are kids starving to death in Africa." I knew this was true because of all the commercials that proved there were kids starving to death in Africa. Now that I am in the last year of my 40's, I still struggle with throwing food away. Anyone that knows me would agree, that does not happen very often. When Mindy and I go out to eat, she knows that when she finishes eating, she slides her plate over to me.

The truth is, most of the people that I know have way more than they could ever need, and that is not just food. That includes all of the other basic stuff that they need to get through life. Since we have so much extra, learning to trust in God for provision is not always the easiest thing to do. The truth is that even though our cabinets and refrigerators are full, if it were not for God, we would all be starving. Sure, we use our paychecks from jobs that we work to buy stuff, but the Lord gives us the strength and ability to do our jobs. Sometimes, we forget that because of how blessed we are.

Learning to trust in God for spiritual provisions is just as difficult sometimes. It may be because we are so used to trying to do things on our own that we forget how much we need Him to provide the things that we need. If He doesn't, I don't care how hard we work, it will never get us where we need to be. As a visionary pastor, God has been doing some things lately, which are reminding me that I must trust in Him to do what I cannot do.

Throughout this book, I have shown you that it is necessary that I have people around me to help me. Sometimes it will be those who help guide me by using constructive criticism, which I gladly welcome. Other times, I need individuals who will use their gifts and callings to actually do the things that need to be done. However, through his word, God revealed to me that we had been recruiting people the wrong way. I will explain this by elaborating on something I mentioned earlier.

On a typical Sunday morning at Delano, or about any other church, there is that awkward time known as "announcements." I do not like that time, but it is a necessary evil. It seems forced and, as my pastor friend Bo says, "There never seems to be the right time to do it." I wholeheartedly agree. I can't tell you how many times we have stood before the church and asked for help in needed positions. It just got to the point where we weren't getting any bites.

Besides the announcements, sign-up sheets have often been a popular means to try to generate interest in getting help. Those things may have been effective in the past, but they don't seem to do anything for us now. I have put sign-up sheets everywhere in the church, and still walk away with no names on them.

Now, let's go back to the chapter before this one. As you will recall, God was challenging me to trust Him, even though people had not been volunteering. Throw into the equation that some people in important positions were leaving the church. This was enough to make anyone question whether the church was going to survive this. It took God bringing a passage to my attention that helped me see what I needed to do.

In Matthew 9:35-38, the Bible says, "Jesus continued going around to all the towns and villages, teaching in their synagogues, preaching the good news of the kingdom, and healing every disease and every sickness. When he saw the crowds, he felt compassion for them, because they were distressed and dejected, like sheep without a shepherd. Then he said to his disciples, 'The harvest is abundant, but the workers are few. Therefore, pray to the Lord of the harvest to send out workers into his harvest'" (CSB). I know I mentioned this passage before, but because of what God is doing at Delano, I felt that it was worth repeating.

When I read this, I realized that I didn't have any other option left. I made announcements and put-up sign-up sheets for people to fill some of these positions before, and some did. Often, they would start and then say that it wasn't for them, or it was not what they thought. I had exhausted all of the options that I was aware of. It was at this point that God's Word hit me like a ton of bricks.

God showed me that Jesus was not instructing His followers to go out and beg people to do things. Because there was a huge harvest, and not enough people, He simply said, "pray to the Lord of the harvest." Wow! How much blood, sweat, tears, and anxiety could we avoid if we would just turn things over to the Lord and let Him bring in the people? It was at this moment that I made the commitment to do just that.

Even though I could share all kinds of ways that God answered this prayer, I want to close this chapter by zoning in on one particular area, the prayer that God would send the people to fill these most critical roles in the church. By bringing in these people, it has given me the opportunity to focus on the things that God has called me to do, and let others do what they are called to do. You will see that these are people that are very gifted, and they have a desire to use those gifts. They are exactly what we needed! Because we waited on the Lord, and He made it happen, the church can fulfill the vision that He has for Delano Baptist.

One of the positions that was essential for us to fill was the youth pastor. For all of its existence, Delano had operated with youth leaders, or directors. Moving in the direction where we would get someone who could be an ordained, associate pastor was the way I felt we should go. I shared it with the deacons, and they were in agreement with me.

One Sunday morning, one of our faithful members, Lynn, told me that he had a distant cousin who was planning on visiting our church. Lynn was on the personnel committee. They were over the hiring of bi-vocational positions. He told me that his cousin was married, and the couple was in their twenties and their names were Jake and Haley.

He told me that Jake was a young preacher and Haley had led worship at their former church. Some things had happened and now they were looking for a new church home. A couple of weeks after he told me about them, they showed up at church.

Two or three days after that service, I got a call from Lynn. He told me that Jake and Haley absolutely loved Delano. Jake had talked about how much he loved everything about the service that day. Lynn told me that it would be a good idea if I called Jake and let him know that we were glad they came, so I did.

When I talked to him, he seemed so excited. He shared with me that they had been in a tough spot lately, and they were looking for a place where they could dig their heels in and get to work. At their former church, they had been doing everything, and I mean everything. Because of that, they almost hit a point of being burned out. I remember him telling me that they wanted to work for the Kingdom, but they did not want to have so much on them that it became miserable. Been there, done that, and it is not fun.

When people tell me that they are interested in the church, or even joining, I have them meet me during Sunday School time. It gives me the time to find out what they are looking for, and how they could fit in. Before we hung up the phone, I suggested that Jake and Haley meet me in the next week or two during Sunday School, and they agreed.

The morning that they came will always be memorable to me. I remember seeing them pull up, and I just felt excited. I didn't know why at the moment, but I would figure it out in the coming months. They walked up, and I was in the middle of a conversation. I told them to step inside, and I would be right there. Within a couple of minutes, I went inside. Someone told me that Pat had taken them over to the youth room, so I went in to talk to them.

When I walked in, Jake and Haley were telling Pat a little about where they had been, and what brought them to Delano. I will never forget what happened when I walked up and stood beside Jake. I sensed a voice. Was it God's voice, my imagination, or what? At the moment I didn't know. The voice said, "There is your youth pastor."

My natural inclination was to scream this out to anyone who would listen. I knew, however, that I needed to keep my mouth shut about this one. I always got myself in trouble every time I jumped into things too quickly, and I had not had time to pray about this. Also, I really didn't know Jake and Haley yet. I do remember that Pat and I had a brief conversation that day after we talked to them. Both of us felt that God was going to do something through them.

I knew I would have to tell Mindy. When we got in the car, I shared with her what happened in the youth room. She did what she normally does, she said, "You need to keep this to yourself for a while and pray about it before you tell anyone else." I agreed with her, and I listened to her, well, pretty much. As I have already said, I am a work in progress.

After some time, we were in a personnel committee meeting. The need for a youth pastor came up, and I shared with the committee about hearing what I believed to be God telling me that Jake would be our youth pastor. I have mentioned Rhonda before and, yet again, she came through with great advice. Her and Mindy think alike when it comes to trying to keep me straight.

Rhonda brought up the fact that we had all jumped into things a little too quickly, in a lot of other situations. Her advice was amazing, and it proved to be spot on. She said this, "Why don't we wait and let the church fall in love with Jake and Haley if this is God's plan." That is exactly what happened. Talk about a self-fulfilled prophecy.

It did not take long for people in the church to fall in love with this couple. I had Jake preach and everyone from the teenagers to the 80-year-olds loved to hear him. Haley started jumping in there and spending time with some of the teenage girls in the church and helping them with the things they were facing in life. It was becoming obvious to everyone around that they were the right fit for this position.

I remember a couple of times people came up to me at church and asked if we had considered Jake for the youth pastor position. It was all I could do to keep my mouth shut about it, but I knew being quiet was what I had to do. God was at work, and I did not want to mess up His plan. It appeared that He had brought us a youth pastor at the perfect time.

Without going into any detail, I will say this. Once we mentioned that we were getting ready to seek out a youth pastor, the enemy reared his ugly head. Boy, did he put up a fight! After dealing with a lot of little battles, it was time for me to meet with the personnel committee about going forward.

Pat was the chairman of the committee and he and I had discussed everything. Both of us felt that Jake was the man, but we had not even formally talked to Jake, nor the committee. I knew that there was a chance that everyone would not be on board. I turned it over to the Lord and trusted that the right decision would be made.

The committee met and Pat got straight to the point. When everyone was there and seated, Pat prayed. After praying he then asked how we needed to proceed. Everyone started talking about how we should announce to the church, as well as social media that we were looking for a youth pastor. Not even five minutes into the discussion, Pat said this, "There is a young couple in the church that I have been thinking about. Do you all know who I'm talking about?" Immediately, everyone said, "yes," and they started discussing how great it would be for Jake to be our youth pastor. That is, if he accepts it.

In the meeting, Pat had even said that he threw a hint out to Jake about the position, and he did not seem interested. After the meeting, Pat went back to Jake and asked him and Haley to pray about this. I texted Jake that night and asked if he would meet me for coffee the next day.

When we met, I asked Jake what the reservations were. He said that Haley was just a little concerned, but it was mainly because she wanted to make sure that this was God leading them. One thing about this couple, they make sure that they are following God. It is not about them. Their humility is one of the things that draws people to them.

As you may have guessed, that was God speaking to me in the youth room. Within a few weeks, Jake was voted in as Delano Baptist Church's first youth pastor. Though it has only been a few months, it has been an amazing ride already. The kids are experiencing spiritual growth in a way that I have never seen them experience before.

This second situation is just as awesome. When I first became the pastor, the church was also in need of a worship leader. Delano has a lot of talented people, who can sing. For those of you who have been in church your entire lives, I know what you are thinking. "Every church brags on their people who sing, whether they are gifted or not." Delano is different. When I say that we have people who can sing, there is no exaggeration at all. When we tell someone that they did a good job, it is not just to encourage; they really did a good job. Since there were so many great singers, the church was using a few of them as interim worship leaders when I became the pastor.

Shortly after I became the pastor, the search began for someone to take the reins. For four years, we struggled in getting, and keeping, this position filled. I will not go into any of the details. I only want you to see how God came through, once I learned to trust His provision. To get the full gist of what God has done, in filling our worship leader position, I have to take you back a few weeks.

As August 2022 was approaching, I sensed God leading me to do something at the church. I felt that we needed to use the month of August to get laser focused on prayer. We did sign-up sheets, for the purpose of accountability. It had 30-minute time slots that people could pray for each day. Also, I opened the church all day on Wednesdays for anyone who wanted to come to the church and pray.

During one of those weeks, I was at the church spending the day in prayer. God brought to my attention something that I had read in a book a few years back. The author talked about how Christians don't spend enough time asking God for, I'll paraphrase, God-sized requests. As I thought about that, an idea came to me. I felt like we needed a room at the church, which would be used only for God-sized requests. If it is going to happen, it will be because God made it happen.

That day, I began walking around the church, and praying over the property, when I noticed a window just above the youth room. I felt drawn to that room, so I went in. God made it very clear to me that this was the place.

Behind our church is the most amazing view of mountains. Just like the time I was in the Atlantic reaching out to God, when I pray about something that I desperately need God to answer, I look at the mountains. It is hard to deny that God can do anything, when you look at His amazing creation. As I stood in that room, I noticed the window. I walked up to it, looked out, and I was staring at the mountains. For me, I knew that this was the place where our room would be. It would be the room where people would pray for things that only God could do.

The very next week, we were again in need of a worship leader. One of our members and deacons is a guy named Josh. For over 20 years he has sung with a quartet. Besides that, he helped fill the worship leader role at church, during times when his group was not singing. In every situation where we had a worship leader leave, Josh has been asked about taking it. Every time, it was the same answer, "I just feel like I am supposed to keep doing what I am doing."

During the week that this position came open, I was doing my quiet time. During that time, I always journal. One morning, I wrote, "God, please show Josh that he is the guy for this position." It was a couple days after that, I talked to him. We were going to need someone to lead the next Sunday morning. Also, it was during that week that personnel were beginning their search for a worship leader. When I asked him he said that he was free that Sunday and could lead.

The day I asked him about it, I said to him, "Josh, I would never ask you to do something that God was not leading you to do. If you are to keep doing what you are doing, I am in full support. But, I would like to ask you to pray about it, just in case." He told me that he would.

For the rest of that week, and up until the next Sunday, I prayed that God would reveal to Josh that this was the position that he was supposed to take. I knew it, everyone in church knew it, but God had to show Josh. On the Wednesday morning, prior to the Sunday that he was going to lead, something hit me. Josh, the personnel committee, and myself needed an answer from the Lord. It was time for us to visit the prayer room. While it was not completely set up yet, the important thing was that we were using it to get in touch with the one who would answer us.

I talked to everyone about meeting together, and they all showed up early on Wednesday. I shared with them all about this room and how God had placed it on my heart. When I say that we had a prayer meeting, I mean heaven came down.

We walked up to the room, and I had everyone just take it all in. They all looked out the window at the mountains. We joined hands and went around the room praying. I heard people pray that I had never heard pray publicly. You could sense the power of the Holy Spirit in every word that came out of their mouths. After we all finished praying, Rhonda, who you have heard about already, broke out with the song, "He is here!" It was one of the most unbelievable moments of prayer that I have ever experienced in a corporate setting.

The stage was now set. Josh, the entire personnel committee, and the pastor had done what we should have done all along. We gave the situation to the Lord, and we trusted that He would do what only

He could do. We had tried things our way for a long time, now it was time to do it right.

I would like to say the next Sunday morning that Josh came in, led, and God showed up in such a way that Josh just had to accept the position that morning. However, it did not happen in that way, but a few things did occur, which showed me that God had this.

First, we had people, who had left the church, come back. Not only were they back, but they were excited about being there again. Then, Josh caught me after service, and he said something to me. It told me that God was at work, and I felt strongly that he would end up taking this position. All he said was this, "I woke up early this morning and couldn't go back to sleep. I got to the church at 7:30, and I went up to the room and prayed." I knew in my heart that the future was about to get very bright at Delano. Not because of anything that we had done, but it was all because we were surrendering to God's will and expecting Him to do what only He could do.

Within a couple of more weeks, Josh let everyone on the committee know that God had opened his heart and was calling him to be the worship leader at Delano. The church was told a few days ago. Just like expected, there were no concerns. Literally, everyone was excited.

When you stop and think about how God brought all of this to pass, it is nothing short of amazing. Only our Lord could work it out so that these kinds of people would end up in the positions that they have. However, that is not the only thing that makes this story great.

These guys are not only a part of the staff that works with me, but they were exactly what I needed as the visionary pastor of Delano. Just like me these guys want to see things happen at the church, for the Kingdom's sake. Unlike how I had been doing things, they are all about doing everything in the Lord's timing and making sure that we have all the right organization to everything that we do. Also, both of them are willing to challenge me when I try to move too fast. I can share my vision with my staff, and they ensure that everything works as it should, and the right people are in place so that it is successful

If your church is having trouble filling the positions that are needed, it is affecting your pastor. He may not show it, but those things always do. Just as you have helped him understand the importance of trusting the process, you also need to guide him in trusting in the Lord's provision. As a visionary, he needs people in place that can help him. People who are wired differently. Remember, all we can do is trust, it is the Lord who will bring it all to pass. Pray for laborers, trust His provision, and watch Him bring the right people at just the right time.

Conclusion

In Paul's letter to the Ephesians, he says something about pastors that you may not have thought much about. In 4:11-13, he lets us know that pastors are actually a gift from God. As a gift to the church, pastors have the ability to train up believers so that they can go on and do ministry, which will, in effect, build up the church. The passage is all about every kind of pastor, even visionaries.

As you have read my story, I hope you have a better understanding of your visionary pastor. I have tried to show you how we think and why we do the things that we do. Also, you have been able to see through my experiences the things that hinder me, as well as those things that strengthen me. Avoiding those things that hinder him, and doing the things that strengthen him, is what your pastor needs.

If he is going to be that leader who equips other believers, he can't do it alone. He needs help and a lot of it. Remember, first and foremost, pray for him! Also, get others on board with you to pray for him. Help him understand the things that I have shared, but do so in a gentle, loving way. Encourage him often, and when you criticize him make sure that it is constructive.

Finally, work with him to make sure others in the church are discipled, so that they will step up and use their gifts and abilities for the advancement of the Kingdom. This really is the way to get the entire body working, so that the pastor doesn't try to carry the entire load. When you have done that, but you still need people, do what Jesus told you to do. Pray for laborers, trust in the process, and trust in His provision!

www.ingramcontent.com/pod-product-compliance
Lightning Source LLC
Chambersburg PA
CBHW071743090426
42738CB00011B/2546